207

A Personal Account of Love, Paranormal Phenomenon and Demonic Possession

JILL MARIE MORRIS

ISBN-10: 146355043X
ISBN-13: 978-1463550431

2041

DEDICATION

For: Mom, Jimmy, Kyle, Carol and Ann.

CONTENTS

PREFACE: *Why now?*

By Jill Marie Morris

This book is a true account of paranormal events that took place in my life between the early summer of 1988, through the late fall of 1989. It is a story of love, faith and tragedy.

I have wanted to share my account for well over two decades, and after many long discussions with family and friends whom were involved with, and bore witness to some of these terrifying events, chose to wait until recently to begin the writing process. Some of this book's content is dramatically unsettling, thus making it understandable as to why I would want to hold off on this venture. More specifically, I wanted to wait until my oldest son was able to grasp, and digest the history, to which this book will reveal.

Undoubtedly, penning this story has been a very cathartic process that has evoked many memories. On the same token, it is by sharing my experiences, that a desire to enlighten and instill hope in spirit, was born.

These events have also made me better realize that from a very young age, *most* people are taught the difference between good and evil, yet often fail to continue educating themselves on such matters, even long after entering adulthood.

Either way, aside from going to church to hear a sermon, or unless occupation, or interest warrant, there is little desire to learn just what evil can encompass in the world around us. I have found this remarkable, considering that I am a fifth generation Spiritual Medium and Clairvoyant who has had to self-tutor on this very topic, in order to better my comprehension of both the physical, and spiritual universe in which we all dwell.

In relationship to the physical and spiritual worlds, I would like to take a moment and ask my readers, how many of you would ever have imagined making a plea for your life, while in the throes of a crisis? I would speculate with fair accuracy, that very few of you have, if any at all.

For all intensive purposes, it seems as though we humans, especially when young, journey through life with an almost invincible and carefree attitude, avoiding such uncomfortable thoughts until we are forced to confront them. Even then, a large number of the people will base their opinions on instinctual fear: A fear of the unknown.

History has proven that there are very few supernatural topics that can generate a high level of panic and fear, as those of demonic oppression, and possession. These incredibly dark and heinous concepts have the ability to make most people question every aspect of their spirituality, from non-believers, to the most devout. I should also mention that for some non-believers such as Atheists, oppression and possession are regarded as more of a psychiatric issue, than anything else.

The topic is open for debate, but for thousands of years, from Shamanism to Catholicism, demonic possession is an intense phenomenon that has a profound and serious need for examination. This book – my story – will give you a first hand look at what it's like to be thrust head first, into a terrifying experience involving a highly probable oppression and possession, linking the events and history, directly to the subject matter.

Devoid of embellishment and exaggeration, and told by

truthful account, through this book I will share with you some of the most intimately painful and horrifying experiences that I have ever encountered. I do so, not for means of gaining sympathy or notoriety, but as a way to educate the general public relative to some very real, and serious issues that many people face, but are too often afraid to discuss. Additionally, I hope to provide insight for my readers, as to what many of us who have an affiliation with the paranormal community, must sometimes deal with.

Considering all of the information and evidence at hand, I will leave you to draw your own conclusion. In turn, I would at least pray that my story will open your minds to better appreciate how sometimes the paranormal realm, can indeed, be a very real part of every day life, whether you initially have chosen to believe it, or not.

"The battle between Good and Evil
Discriminates no quest for arena
Nor portends before it begins,
But the power to stand
On the side of what's Godly
Through strength in spirit
Will assure His win."

                            ~ Jill Marie Morris

Please note that some of the names of the individuals mentioned in this book have been changed to protect their privacy and identity. Thank you.

INTRODUCTION

Granville, New York
(1970)

With the smell of fresh lilacs wafting gently through the summer air, the little girl looked up at her grandmother as she carefully inserted newly snipped blooms into a bucket of water sitting on the ground. "Gram?" the little girl asked as she bent over, pressing her nose against a stem. "Do angels have fluffy, white wings?"

"Most of them do. Why do you ask?" replied the grandmother, as she continued to select the purple hued treasures from a hanging limb.

"I was wondering if I'm gonna get to have big, fluffy, white wings, too. Angels are so beautiful!" the little girl gushed.

"Well dear, you have quite a bit of time before you have to worry about getting your angel wings, but when you do, I'm sure they will be magnificent. For now, you can be my pretty, little Living Angel. How does that sound?" the grandmother commented, handing the little girl some more specimens. "Would you like to help carry the bucket of flowers into the house for me?"

"I suppose," answered the little fair-haired girl. Brushing off a few straggling leaves that were dangling from her sundress, the child skipped between the tree and the bucket of flowers. "All angels are good. I'm going to be a *really* good Living Angel and carry the flowers for you, okay, Gram?"

Stopping for a moment to examine the enthusiasm on her granddaughter's face, she noticed how innocent and happy the child was. "You know dear, you are a very good girl but not all angels are nice," she replied.

The child glanced at her grandmother with a look of disappointment on her face. "What do you mean not all angels are nice?" she asked in concern.

Seeing her granddaughter struggle to lift the water-laden bucket, the grandmother tipped it towards one side, allowing some of the water to spill out onto the green grass. "There are good people, and there are bad people in the world; the same applies to angels. You see, sometimes a good angel falls out of Heaven and lands in a very scary place, making them a bad angel," the grandmother explained.

The little girl's eyes grew wide. "Oh, no! Bad angels sound *really* scary!" the little girl shuddered in concern.

"They can be," responded the grandmother, as she placed another lilac branch in the girl's small hand. "Do you know what they call bad angels?" asked the grandmother, as she handed the stem to the girl.

"No," the little girl quietly answered, staring up at her grandmother in anticipation.

"A bad angel is called a Fallen Angel," she advised.

"Are Fallen Angels *really, really* bad?" the child asked as she watched the emptied water soak into the ground. "Can they ruin our flowers?"

"Yes, they are very, very bad and I suppose they could ruin our flowers, but God is protecting them, just like he is protecting you, every day," she said in a reassuring tone.

With the water decreased by half, the bucket was then more manageable for the young child to bring to the house. "Why don't you give a try?" the grandmother suggested. "It should be much easier for you to carry now."

Lifting the bucket with all of her might, the little girl

squealed in delight as she and her grandmother walked up the slate pathway to the front of the house. With her grandmother holding the porch door open, the little girl cautiously proceeded into the house, her prized lilacs in tow.

"Gram, will God protect me from Fallen Angels for my whole life?" she asked while carefully pushing the bucket onto the kitchen table.

Taking a large, glass vase from the oak trimmed cupboard, the grandmother answered, "Yes, dear. God and his good angels will always watch over you and protect you from the Fallen Angels. Now stop worrying your pretty little head over such things and help Grandma put these beautiful flowers in the vase."

1

Clown & Muse

Nestled amidst the rolling, green hills of eastern Rensselaer County in New York State, rests my Alma Mata: Tamarac High School. Sprawling across several acres, surrounded by dairy farms and crystal clear lakes, its student body is a healthy blend of both suburban and rural families.

With a curb appeal that maintains a more wholesome profile, it is home to some of the most endearing memories of my youth. A reminder of my love for the countryside, it is also reminiscent of how the surrounding areas of Brunswick, Eagle Mills, Pittstown, Raymertown, Cropseyville, Boyntonville and Grafton, lent its town folk as the threads that have woven my metaphorical, and warm quilt of friendship.

Through long hallways, intimate classroom settings and fresh country air (unless the winds shifted, carrying a reminder of the local chicken farm), I fondly recollect many an anecdote that I have had the great pleasure of being able to share with my own children. Tamarac High School was not just an educational institution; it was like a large home filled with extended family members, each unique in character. Even today, I consider my closest childhood friends to be family, stemming from a bond that began to grow in 1979.

My first husband Jim and I had initially met in high school, back in the early '80's. Although two years older than I, we found ourselves struggling through the same Math class. Talkative, friendly, incredibly handsome and quite the prankster, he had recently transferred to our small school, after having gone to live with foster parents.

Quite frequently, I would spend most of the time in class dividing my attention between the lessons being taught and plucking rubber bands, wads of paper and other assorted objects cast in negative attention, out of my meticulously coiffed hair. Never hostile, Jim's intentions were that of a typical teenaged boy, attempting to gain the attention of an adolescent girl. Regardless, I remember it being incredibly distracting – and quite annoying.

Admittedly, Jim's tall stature, combined with his ability to befriend even the toughest kid in school, was a bit intimidating to me. He definitely had a hefty dose of rebel in his genes and that was as obvious to me, as the nose on my face. Having been raised the daughter of a New York State Trooper I typically tended to shy-away from his type. As comical and charming as he could certainly be, everyone knew that you didn't fool around with Jim.

Nonetheless, Jim's boyish antics verged on entertaining. They certainly perked up a rather boring class. Funny to look back at the dynamics that were at play, for as the saying goes: Good girls are typically attracted to bad boys. Everyone in the class knew that he was a clown, and I was his Math Muse.

I will never forget the time that he asked if I had a boyfriend. How I would have loved to say, "Yes," but meekly forced out a, "No."

His response only made me feel even more uncomfortable. Not settling for my answer, he further antagonized me by asking me to elaborate as to why I did not have one. Bashfully replying with an, "I don't know," I felt the humiliating sensation that my face and entire body, were turning beet red. *How embarrassing.*

Listening intently with an impish smile, he then asked if I would consider being his girlfriend, by which I quickly declined, trying to focus on the less social aspects of class. Insistent, he continued to jibe me.

I remember how this was such a strange predicament for me to be in the midst of. As much as he annoyed the snot out of me, I was actually attracted to him. Intrigued and repulsed, I knew that I had to keep my distance.

Unfolding in a rather awkward sort of way, the situation had grown more uncomfortable. I can clearly recall the look on his face when I declined him as a suitor, wondering if I had actually hurt his feelings.

Rather than get into any more trouble for the off-topic, non-mathematical related conversations, I thought that it would be a good idea to move my seat, understanding fully well that by doing so, I was committing an official act of snobbery. Still, the calculated swapping of desks took the fun out of math for Jim, as I was then too far away for target practice.

Of course that did not entirely stop him, as I would occasionally hear his taunts and have to dodge some type of flying object when the teacher turned their head. Regardless, changing spots managed to be a strategically successful endeavor.

Such as high school life seems to be riddled with change, be it fair-weather friends, crushes and fads, Jim slowly disappeared off the radar. It wasn't long before is presence was neither seen, nor heard in the school hallways.

I remember a mutual acquaintance had informed me that Jim had left his foster parents, and had returned home to Troy. Math class was once again uneventful, and painfully boring.

* * * * * * *

Memorial Day weekend was always a special time for my paternal grandmother Meme, and I. For almost every year since

I was a young child, we would sit on her front steps, dressed in our red, white and blues to watch Rensselaer's Memorial Day parade.

Meme would pull out all of the stops by providing a host of unhealthy comfort foods, fit for fat royalty. I fondly remember the excitement and anticipation of her spread, most looking forward to her small, crystal bowls filled with sparkling gumdrops, funky little orange, peanut-shaped, marshmallow confections, mounds of buttery popcorn and a tray of precisely cut pizza squares, all carefully arranged on the table with her special holiday tablecloth. Even if the guest list was limited to just my brother and I, the day remained a big to-do.

Considering that I was a young adult in May of 1986, it was not the food or festivities that mattered the most for the holiday weekend, but the time that Meme and I would have to spend together. It had become one of our special bonding experiences, and that year in particular, I was looking especially forward to visiting with her.

Originally, I did not think that I would be able to make the trip, but due to a last-minute change of plans (such is the life of a twenty-year-old), I managed to navigate my way to my grandmother's in hopes of spending a few relaxing days with her. Upon arrival, she greeted me in her festive garb and we immediately began catching up with the latest on life, inclusive of getting what I would later refer to, as her "Celebrity Scoop." Meme absolutely loved the tabloids, with each and every one of them existing as an integral part of her reading repertoire. She would sit for hours on end, pouring over every last article she could get her hands on, swaying to and fro in her rocking chair, periodically chuckling, or making an exclamation of disapproval.

Another customary event while visiting, regardless of holiday, was her nap. Rising at the crack of dawn each day without fail, she would escape into catnap mode come early afternoon.

Given the festivities of the day, she was a little more tired than usual. It had come to me as no surprise when she suggested that I take one of her folding chairs and sit in the sun while she had her siesta.

Off I went to soak up the rays on the old, wooden patio in hopes of enjoying a bit of fresh air and a few private moments of tranquility. Little did I know, that any prior idea I had considered of attaining that tranquility, would quickly take a back seat after venturing out onto the porch.

Shortly after setting up camp, I noticed that my grandmother's neighbors had just commenced a rather large Memorial Day party. Not having an issue with the party itself, it was more bothersome to me that my position on the second floor put me in direct view of the celebration. Oh, the joy! I remember hoping that they wouldn't notice me.

So there I sat, dressed in my favorite denim shorts and a red and white t-shirt, hair fashioned into a ponytail, scrunched into the corner. Sticking my face up towards the sun, I recall feeling very happy that I was with my grandmother. Not only was it a perfect afternoon, but the party was providing me with the ability to listen to some great classic rock by Fleetwood Mac and the Eagles, that was booming from a makeshift DJ table.

Lost in the music, and warmed by the golden rays, I had just about dozed-off when I heard my grandmother's neighbor call up to me. Squinting through the sun's glare, I remember glancing down towards the property line, seeing her hand waving back and forth in order to get my attention.

Acknowledging her gesture and waving back, I responded with a courteous, "Hi." She then asked if I wanted to come down to the party to meet *someone*. I politely declined, but was met with a series of jeers and short whistles, flowing out of the mouths of a small group of young men who had gathered near the fence.

Due to the direction of the sun in relationship to my view, I recall that I could not quite discern the young bucks, but do remember having considered a retreat into the house. Instead, I relinquished a girlish giggle, and resumed my sun experience. Within a few minutes, the whistles and jeers had come to a halt.

I remember returning to the house to have dinner with my

grandmother. Being rather tickled by the events, she felt that I was being too shy and needed to get out and meet people. I begged to differ, stating that other than her two adult neighbors, I had no idea who those people were, and was not about to venture over alone, especially due to the large quantities of 'adult beverages' that were visibly flowing like the nearby Hudson River, itself.

They say timing is everything, and so was the case when shortly after Meme's lecture, a knock came upon her door. Staying in the living room, my grandmother got up to answer it, returning with her long-time neighbor, followed by a very tall man. It didn't take long until he came into focus, when I all but fell off of my grandmother's worn, olive green sofa. *It was Jim!*

I could not believe my eyes – or my ears! Entering her parlor, he was chuckling with the same laugh I recalled from Math class. Meme's neighbor then formally introduced me to Jim.

Grinning from ear to ear, his immediate reaction was to ask if I remembered him. Other than sporting a different, more contemporary hairstyle, he looked exactly the same. I was flabbergasted!

My grandmother's neighbor then went on to explain that Jim had recognized me when I had gone out to sit in the sun, earlier in the day. She also advised me that it was Jim, who had wanted to catch my attention. The whistling, the laughter, the group of young men at the fence – it all made sense at that point.

Meme was thrilled with the discovery, and a bit more so than I. After another invite by the neighbor to go join the festivities, I begrudgingly obliged and sauntered over to socialize with the crowd. It was time to mingle.

I fondly recall taking advantage of the opportunity to tease Jim about the times he had pelted me with rubber bands and paper wads. Flashing a big smile, he assured me that he had left them behind.

One rather funny memory that I have of that day was when my grandmother had sternly warned Jim to behave. She had no idea what he was capable of, more so relative to taunting. Ironically though, Jim managed to be a perfect gentleman.

I later returned to my grandmother's and found her anxiously rocking back in forth in her chair; she wanted the scoop. Detailing the events of the night, I told her how much more mature Jim seemed to be in comparison to the time we spent together at Tamarac High School. Much to her fancy, I also admitted there was some type of spark.

That was when my grandmother's face lit up; she was thrilled! Making light of her suggesting that he "could be the one," I readied for bed and fell asleep wondering if perhaps, she was right. Stranger things had happened.

Jim and I dated two more times over the course of the following month. Through time, be it by coincidence or fate, we became inseparable. He fast became my best friend. Incredibly funny and remarkably caring, I remember thinking that his heart was as big as an ocean.

Another fond memory that I have of Jim pertains to something that I have often told my son about, as strangely enough, he does the *same thing*. At times, when listening to music, Jim would burst into song - always in the most inappropriate of places. Bless his heart: I sadly recall that he could not carry a tune to save his life. He was truly tone deaf.

Without a care in the world, he would serenade me with hilarious lyrics, which were a blend of both the original song, and of his own devise. He always knew how to make me smile and let me know how much he loved me. The Class Clown had become my Knight In Shining Armor.

Despite our hugely different backgrounds, we got along wonderfully. I was incredibly happy, as was my mother and his family for us, though my relationship with my father had pretty much disintegrated by then.

I cannot remember why, but several months before our wedding, Jim had lost his job as a Cook at the Watervliet Arsenal. I was then the sole breadwinner, working full time as a Registration Clerk at a local hospital. Ever the handyman, Jim was able to find seasonal work as a Painter and carried on, making a decent living.

After saving up for our wedding, Jim and I were married in September of 1987. We were both elated and eager to start a family, which was something we had often discussed, and looked very forward to. Shortly thereafter, we moved into our own apartment, and embarked upon our lives as husband and wife – but not without enduring some hardship.

Come that following October, just over a month after we married, I found out that I was pregnant. My due-date: June 18th, 1988.

The excitement was somewhat subdued to the fact that Jim wanted to find a more stable job, doing what he knew and loved; cooking. Facing parenthood, the situation seemed to prompt him into realizing that he needed to buckle-down. That was when he found a job working as a Cook at the locally famous South End Tavern, a very well known eatery situated just before the Menands Bridge, in Troy.

No sooner did Jim begin his new job, than we suffered yet another blow, as I miscarried very early into the pregnancy. Jim and I were devastated. I had a very difficult time coping with the miscarriage and emotionally, as well as spiritually, took things incredibly hard.

Encouraging me to speak with our priest, Jim wanted to help me, but felt as though his hands were tied. Father was a kind and sincere man; however, it was such a profoundly personal experience, that I could not connect with him on the level that I needed. Regardless, I have a beautiful memory of Jim that took place on the night we walked from the rectory, back to the church parking lot, after speaking with Father about the miscarriage.

Feeling as though nobody understood what I had been going through, I stopped and burst into tears, under a beautiful night sky. To lose a child, even at such an early stage, was unbelievably overwhelming. Understanding my fragile emotional state, Jim wrapped his long, lanky arms around me in comfort, and promised that he would always be there for me – for us. His love and compassion were what I loved so very much about him. Taking the time to comfort me in that moment of need had meant the world. Together we cried, as the twinkling stars above, encouraged a sense of hope.

Soon after recovering, and right after Christmas of 1987, Jim and I received some wonderful news; I was once again expecting. The timing seemed to be close to perfect; all that we needed was to move closer to our jobs. It was quite difficult commuting in two different directions with the means of one vehicle. Blessed, we knew what we had to do to ensure a safe and viable pregnancy, and began planning a move towards the end of our existing lease. Fortunately, our lease would end prior to my August 21st, 1988, due-date.

* * * * * * *

1988 began on a good note; my pregnancy was progressing without issue, and I was healthy. I also managed to avoid any bought of morning sickness, and was looking very forward to motherhood.

Late winter and spring of that year will forever be one of the happiest periods in my life. With an impending lease renewal, we knew we had to make a move that would be more suitable to our needs. Jim assured me that he had things under control and knew of a few individuals that had properties for rent. The only glitch that I recall, was the fact that I began to have a very strange series of dreams shortly before we began to look for the new apartment.

No sooner had we commenced our hunt, than one of Jim's contacts invited him to go look at a large flat in Watervliet. It had certainly seemed like a good fit, but from the onset of mentioning this apartment, something did not sit right with me.

After voicing my concerns to my husband about this oddity, he convinced me to at least give it a look, as the price and location were 'right.' He also told me that the house happened to be next door to the home of our close friends Len and Sarah; Sarah would eventually be babysitting our child, no matter where we decided to move. I remember thinking that it was worth the effort, but due to the uneasy feeling that I had about the property, I asked Jim if he and Len would take a first peek, to which they agreed.

Returning from his meeting with the Landlord, Jim was very enthusiastic, stating that it was a fantastic apartment. Aside from any attempt to make it sound appealing, I simply could not visualize living there.

Quite an unusual feeling, I would not deem it bad, but did not consider it good. I was less than thrilled about my gut feeling, and had a tough time seriously considering the option. So tough in fact, Len called and urged me to go check it out.

Much to my chagrin, I decided to move forward with a tour. After visiting the flat, we would have dinner at Len and Sarah's.

Approximately five months pregnant, I had to focus on nesting, and getting a new home in order for the arrival of our baby. Moving to Watervliet meant a good deal to Jim, and given the fact he had made some very valid points in his argument to relocate there, I had to give it a go.

2

First Impressions

Watervliet, New York is small city that is situated just to the north of Albany. First settled in 1643, it became somewhat of a hub for a rudimentary ferry system used to cross the Hudson River between Albany, and Rensselaer counties during the Revolutionary War. A more notable aspect of the ferry was that it had been used as a means of transporting troops for the Battle of Saratoga, in 1777.

Throughout history, Watervliet, and much of the surrounding area including the City of Troy, flourished, gaining a reputation as one of many manufacturing towns along the Hudson River. By the 19th Century, and due in part to its strategic shipping location, several commercial manufacturing industries had sprouted up, in full force.

Perhaps one of the most distinguished points of interest in the history of Watervliet, is a section of land originally purchased by the Federal Government, circa 1813, which later became home to the Watervliet Arsenal. Listed as one of the nation's oldest manufacturers of tanks, mortars and artillery for the United States Army, the Arsenal was constructed specifically to support the War of 1812, and remains both open and operational, to-date.

Given the very rich history of the surrounding area, it was only natural to see residences and other small businesses prosper along the main thoroughfare. As the city continued to expand, the streets became lined with an eclectic blend of architectural styles spanning from as early as the late 18th Century, through current day.

19th Street, initially established as Genesee Street, and now known as NY Route 2, runs in an east-west direction. The Congress Street Bridge, which crosses the Hudson River into Troy, is located at its most easterly point, intersecting with 2nd Avenue. Heading west from the bridge, 19th Street runs uphill, towards the village of Latham. This roadway is quite popular even today, for travelers seeking alternate routes to avoid congestion on the more popular NY I-87, and NY I-787.

Specifically, 207 19th Street was snuggly situated on the north side of 19th Street, mere yards west of the intersections of 19th Street, and 2nd Avenue. It was a soaring structure amongst a row of homes built during various time periods, beginning in the mid-to-late 1800's.

Various family businesses line the street, some of which have been long established. Considered a safe area at the time, the aspect of security was never an issue to consider.

207's most immediate neighbors included a family owned and operated Pizza Parlor located directly across the street, with a small business to the left of 207, and a single-family residence to its right. It was a decent and convenient location to live; however, my reluctance had little to do with location, so much as it did with the actual property itself.

As it were, I would liken my willingness to view the flat, even after coming to an agreement of participation, to that of going to a dentist to have a root canal. I knew that it was something that I needed to do, but procrastinated about it, and put off for as long as I could. No matter how many times that Jim and Len tried to 'sell it,' I could not shake the feeling.

In spite of that, I sucked it up and went along for the ride, with hope that they would at least stop nagging me about it.

On the day of our arrival, Jim and I had parked in Len's driveway. Len and Sarah's property was situated to the rear, or north side of, and perpendicular to, 207. Their lengthy yard extended directly behind the flat in an east-west direction.

From my initial glance up towards 207 from the view of Len's driveway, I immediately noted its size; it towered over the structures situated within the immediate area. I could also see that an addition had been built onto the back of the property, occurring quite a long while after the home's original construction.

Having picked up the keys earlier, Jim and I were greeted by Len. We then took a quick walk around the back of the property, passing through the small backyard and circling around to the front entrance, located on 19th Street. I remember the quiet intensity of the building.

Even with its cleanliness, I did not have a positive psychic feeling about the exterior. It had a very cold, austere feeling to it, and regardless of the fact that the brick had a somewhat fresh coat of blood red paint, its black star-shaped ornamental plaques, contrasted the color in quite a creepy fashion.

Perhaps the most peculiar aspect about the building, was that the property and building were not parallel to the street like its neighbors, but were situated on a diagonal. Instead of having a direct north-south orientation, 207 had been built on a more northwest-southeasterly axis.

I recall that from a psychic perspective, it had truly bothered me, but since Len was accompanying us, Jim had asked me to withhold commentary until after we returned home. This was hard for me to do, as even before I had a chance to go into the building, I wanted to turn around and go home. With an open mind, yet still harboring reservation, we climbed a few gray, concrete steps, and entered the house.

The large wood framed doors were heavy; their windows covered with brittle, off-white shades, and a slightly worn pair of sheer panels. They were almost ghostly, in appearance.

Once inside, the entrance to the first floor flat was to the right. To the left, was a large, dark brown, wooden banister that rose upwards to the second, and third floor units. Well-maintained, the interior décor was lacking style, dating back to the late 1950's-early 1960's. There had been no recent modernization efforts, aside from the exterior paint job.

Touching the weathered banister, a small jolt of energy, much like a zap of static electricity – only stronger – shot into my right hand and traveled up my arm. Startled, I recall jumping just enough that it prompted Jim to be concerned that I had tripped, or had lost my balance. Continuing to hold onto the rail, the sensation did not last for more than a couple of seconds.

The staircase was straight, steep and narrow. Every step we climbed seemed to relinquish a creak; like an eerie and aged tune. I recall trying to visualize the home and the grandeur of the staircase in its original state, yet could not. The plain walls were a dark, teal green, trimmed with a moderately preserved, rich brown, crown molding. The light fixtures appeared to be quite old: The faded brass sconces presented an oxidized, greenish tone, lending them to have a wraithlike feel.

Adding to an increasing sense of anxiety, the closer I became to the door at the top of the stairs, the more I could not help but feel that I was slowly entering another dimension. Step by step, it was as if being sucked into a vacuum of time. The air became heavier, and there seemed to be a sense of finality when looking up towards it. By far, this was not a good omen, but I was sworn to silence.

Creak – groan – creak – groan – the aching sounds of the aged wood floorboards resonated years of repressed pain from the belly of the old house. It was *strange*.

Fortunately, the lock and key systems on the exterior and interior doors were somewhat updated, although just moments before entering 207, I half expected Jim to pull out a huge, iron skeleton key from his pocket. It would have fit perfectly into the ambiance that the house exuded. Within a quick twist of the key in lock, and after taking a deep breath, the three of us were standing in the dining room of the flat.

From most angles, the apartment appeared to be very spacious. On the east side of the dining room, were two doors that converged into the master bedroom. To the north, or rear of the flat, was the kitchen.

Showing me the master bedroom first, Jim and Len described that two small rooms had been turned into one large bedroom, thus the explanation for having two entry doors separated by a matter of 10 feet, or so. The size of the room was more than sufficient, and the lighting very good. The whitewashed paneling would be more of an adjustment, than anything else.

Looking around the bedroom, I remember noticing some personal items in boxes, scattered about the room. It looked as if someone had not quite finished moving out.

Returning to the dining room, I immediately walked towards the kitchen in the back of the house. That was when Jim and Len asked where I was going.

Questioning why their voices had trailed away from me, I swung around, noticing that they had looped back through the dining room and were standing in a room that I had *not* noticed: The living room.

The room was enormous! Jim even remarked at how obvious the gigantic archway was to the room, adding that someone would have to be blind to miss it. Frankly, I could not quite understand how I had managed to do so.

I remember my husband making a goofy remark about my pregnancy being the cause to my 'poor eyesight,' and then he and Len enjoying a hearty laugh, at my bewildered expense. Looking back, I know that I was 'blocking' it.

Completely turning myself around, I headed into the bright, chartreuse colored room, where I noticed a strange haze hanging in the air. I would best describe this as looking through a very misty film covering the lens of a camera. Mentioning this haze to both Jim and Len, they did not understand what I was talking about.

Continuing with the tour of the over-sized living room, I

noted two, very tall windows overlooking 19th Street, which provided a great deal of sunlight in the afternoon. On the east wall was a large, wood framed fireplace and mantel with painted brick inlay. The entire room seemed like a hodge-podge of different decorative time periods, in dire need of a makeover.

After remarking about having to repaint the room if we were to move in, I noticed the center part of the floor, which appeared to have had some type of damage to it. Upon closer inspection, a large patch of the blonde hardwood floor had recently been stripped – the section that had been sanded was somewhat circular in shape, approximately 5' in diameter. The dust and debris from the floor's old varnish had settled haphazardly about the room; the sanding equipment left to the side, leaning against the north wall.

I also remember seeing a few more boxes of personal belongings grouped together, to the left of the fireplace. I couldn't help but wonder what had happened to the floor. Jim must have noticed my expression as I gazed down: He advised me that the former Tenant had spilled some paint. In turn, he stated the Landlord was trying to strip the area and refinish the surface of the floor.

Paint? The room had not seen a new coat of paint since the 1960's! I clearly recall that something was not adding up.

He then told me that the floors were dry and overdue for a poly coating. Upon his original meeting with the Landlord, Jim explained that he had offered to complete the flooring project for the entire room. Apparently the Landlord had offered to forego the security deposit, or part of it, in exchange for Jim's services. A considerate gesture, I still could not understand what would have caused someone to focus on the middle of the floor and just leave it in that condition, plus, I did not see a single drop of paint anywhere around the area in question.

Unsure as to what really had happened, I did make a comment about possibly using the dining room as the living room because the front room bothered me. As far as Jim was concerned, that was not an option. He did, however, promise to paint the living room before he finished the floors, stating that he would make it look like a brand new room. I remember thinking; nope, that's not going to make a difference.

Heading back towards the kitchen, I inspected the heating unit on the west wall of the dining room. It was embellished with two small, gas pipes. The component was situated in front of a non-functional fireplace and mantel. A boon to look at, it relinquished decorative ironwork to detract from its obvious purpose. While turning towards the back of the flat, something on the dark, hardwood floor had managed to catch my eye.

Looking down, I noticed two small, approximately size 7 shoe prints, leading from the living room, into the dining room, turning towards the entrance to the apartment. The shoe prints looked as if someone had walked through a very dark stain, and had never bothered to clean them up. The prints resembled what I would refer to as an "old fashioned" type of shoe, with block heels and pointed toes. Surprised, I asked Jim and Len if they could figure out their cause.

Their story: Someone was probably staining the dining room unaware that they had stepped in the stain and later applied a darker coat of polyurethane to cover the prints. I remember questioning how someone could not notice two sets of footprints, but was met with resistance and didn't challenge their explanation.

That was when I recall being overcome with nausea. Not accustom to morning sickness, I recall feeling slightly shaky, and quite sick to my stomach.

I remember asking both of them point-blank, if someone had died in the flat, or house, by which they laughed and swore on their lives that nobody had. I told them that things were not sitting right with me and took the opportunity to ask why the former Tenant had left the house.

Len, sensing that I was getting upset, interrupted Jim, stating that the former Tenant had taken off without notice due to personal reasons. Jim added that the Landlord would have the items removed and the flat cleaned, prior to the arrival of the new Tenants.

Grilling Jim further, I remember asking if he was trying to cover for a shady Landlord, to which he and Len insisted that the Landlord was fine, and that nothing sinister had happened on the property. They could say what they wanted, but I recall the fact that my psychic senses were telling me something completely different. Between the heaviness in the air, the fact that I missed an entire room, along with the overall creepy house vibes, the flat's aura was quite disconcerting.

After Jim spent a few minutes calming me down, we proceeded towards the back of the house where the kitchen, bathroom and second bedroom, were situated. I remember feeling a rush of heat hit me, as we walked to the next room.

As far as I was concerned, the flat was no longer a choice – I really wanted nothing to do with it. From the get-go, it felt as though I was walking into a psychic Disney Land full of crazy secrets, all contained in one massive, haunted, brick mansion – and no particular spirit energies had even presented at that point.

Wanting to finish the tour quickly, we moved from the dining room into the kitchen. Knowing that the rear of the flat was an addition, I remember how surprised I was when stepping over the threshold; it was like transitioning into yet another time zone.

I recall a strange undertone that permeated the air, noticing that it was quite a bit lighter in comparison to the front of the house. Knowing that this was the area of the flat where I would be spending most of my time, I thought it acceptable and neat in appearance. It had a large, north-facing kitchen window, which overlooked Len and Sarah's house, and yard.

I also remember being taken-back by something that jumped out, relative to my sixth sense. It was not so much the back of the flat that bothered me, but the distant view, just *beyond* Len and Sarah's.

Situated to the northwest, I picked up on a rather dark energy that seemed to encompass that general corner of the cityscape. The immediate view was fantastic, but the direction beyond, was tainted by a disruption in energy; it was almost black! That area harbored something bad, but it was the least of my concerns at the time.

Still not enough to sway my opinion on the flat as whole, the addition was like a breath of fresh air in comparison to the front. The kitchen was more than adequate and roomy. The second bedroom, which would be the baby's nursery, was airy, bright and large.

With Jim and Len repeatedly questioning how I felt, I withheld comment, all the while asking myself if the move was really worth taking a chance. Something was very *wrong* in the front part of the house.

Even if the apartment was going to receive a new coat of paint and Jim was to repair the floor in the front room, I did not think that it would work out. Whatever I had picked up on did not seem like typical spiritual energy. It was … *different*.

Up to that day, I had never felt anything like it beforehand. It was as if something was trying to manifest, but had not. It seemed weak, but nonetheless present; just enough to let me know that it was there. Looking back, that was a *huge* clue.

Exiting the apartment and giving one last look into the living room, I could still see the haze. I did not like 207 at all, and a large part of the aversion had to do with that room.

During dinner, I remember asking Sarah about her opinion of the flat. She stated that she had never had a chance to go inside. A native of the area, I then asked if she knew if the house had any type of history and responded to me by stating that nothing in particular stuck out in her mind. She did, however, mention that she knew the prior Tenant had left abruptly, due to some type of personal situation, just as her husband Len, had stated.

Shooting from the hip, I told the three of them that I was uneasy about it. Jim's frown had made it clear that he disapproved of my judgment. I left it at that, resuming the conversation on the way home, in the car.

I explained to Jim that my first impression of the house was not a good one, and gave him the supporting evidence as to why I had felt that way. I also remembering telling him about the brief jolting sensation when I had touched the banister on the way up the stairs: He, himself, saw my abrupt movement and thought I was going to fall. He couldn't deny that.

I also argued the fact that I managed to 'miss' the very obvious living room, in addition to noticing the mist, the peculiar and partially stripped floor, the footprints in the dining room, and the weird separation of energy that existed between the front and rear sections of the house. Tossing in the fact that the prior Tenant took off in the middle of the night, what person wouldn't think something was up? It was very unsettling.

Jim's viewpoint was one that was obviously less emotional than mine. He did agree that the entire picture was a bit different, but also suggested that my pregnancy had put me in a heightened state of sensitivity. He also weighted his argument on the cost-effective aspects of the move, in addition to the abbreviated commute and logistics of Sarah living right next door, to care for the baby.

Collectively, he made a good case. After going around and around for two days, I finally succumbed to his quest for the flat, and agreed to the move. I was not happy about it, but my husband was.

And so, having to paint the walls and finish the living room floor prior to move-in, the scheduled date to take occupancy at 207 19th Street, was slated for 30 days later. During that time, something told me to pray – hard. Uneasy about the choice, I had no idea that it would become one of the most dangerous decisions that either one of us would ever make.

3

Dream Sequencing

Be it the result of fluctuating pregnancy hormones, or the anticipation of the move, I began having some very unusual (yes, even for me), dreams just prior to looking at the flat at 207. What made them so peculiar was the fact that they would continue where the prior had left off. Rarely dreaming on consecutive nights, or in sequence, a serious of a dozen or so small dreams, took place that left me suspicious as to their cause.

The dreams began with me pregnant and crying: I remember feeling very alone, as though Jim had abandoned me. Wandering through an unidentifiable area of yellow fog, I would call out my husband's name, while holding my swollen belly. Upon waking, I recall a sense of relief, as I would reach over and put my arm around him, eventually floating back to sleep.

I also remember asking some of my 'mom friends' if they had ever experienced strange dreams during their pregnancies. Of little consolation, some stated that they had them, but nothing quite like mine. Most offered advice that they would more than likely stop within a short period of time. As far I as was concerned, that could not happen soon enough.

The series of dreams seemed to be similar to my 'premonition' dreams, yet unique in the fact that there was nothing to 'read' other than my emotions. Another contrast was that a premonition dream would, and still does, carry a specific feeling with detailed clues or symbols, to assist in decoding the actual vision. Upon onset, the new dreams offered little else to go by for interpretation.

Every night, the dreams intensified presenting new emotions, which further confused me. The next few dreams, however, took a dramatic turn, becoming more nightmarish.

I recall asking Jim where he had gone and why he had deserted me, but his entire demeanor had changed. He then began driving me around in the car, like a raging lunatic. At one point, I woke up crying in fear, thinking that I was actually in the car with him!

Initially, I did not tell Jim about the dreams. Upsetting him was to be avoided at all costs, if possible, and were far too difficult, to explain. Noticeable, was the fact that the dreams did increase in frequency and severity, just prior to, and right after moving into the new apartment. By far, the last two were the most troubling.

Approaching my third trimester, I was feeling very well aside from the nightly interruptions. The only thing that I could correlate the nightmares to was my anxiety about the move; however, no matter how hard I tried, I could not relax.

On the fence about the whole situation, I kept it to myself and did what I thought was in the best interest for Jim, and I. While the dreams hinted an indication of premonition, I would try to put them out of mind. Suffice to say; I will never forget the last night we spent in our old apartment, prior to moving in to 207.

The dream began the same: Alone, then kidnapped and being held hostage in the car by Jim. However, during this vision, he had transformed into a very bizarre looking animal.

He had horns, sharp teeth and was frenzied. I remember screaming and begging him to stop the car and let me out. I also remember the look in his eyes; it was as if his soul was replaced with that of a *monster*. His physical body was driving the car, but a fiend was inside of him, snarling and gnashing at me.

Hysterical in dream, I woke up screaming for him to stop. As a result, I scared the living dickens out of my sleeping husband. Waking to my screams, Jim had no idea what was going on and had thought that I was being attacked. Quite understandably, he was upset upon learning that I was having one hell of a nightmare.

After waking up from that dream, I began to have Braxton-Hicks contractions, and was afraid that the stress of the dream had caused me to go into premature labor. Calling my mother for advice, she had Jim time the contractions over the telephone. Gradually, they stopped and we eventually settled back down.

With a concerned Jim at my side, he urged me to disclose the dream details. As not to cause him too much concern, I thought it best to abridge the night terror, telling him that I was in a car with a monster and wanted to get out. Always trying to make me laugh when I was having an off moment, he told me to stop eating so many peppers, cheese and crackers, which was my one and only craving during the pregnancy.

I can still recall hearing him try to correlate the peppers I had digested, with the monster – it was actually quite hilarious. His silliness helped me relax enough to get some sleep. It had been a very stressful night.

I was rather exhausted the next day, but thanks to help from Jim and his friends, I had to do very little, other than to direct our moving crew as to where to put our furniture and boxes. Rightfully worried about my getting a good night's rest, Jim decided that we would spend the night at his parents' house and return to the new place with a fresh start. Since the move was over, I was hoping and praying that my 'fright-mares' would stop.

23

* * * * * * *

The first night in the apartment was restfully peaceful, although earlier in the day, I had spent quite a bit of time studying the footprints that were permanently ingrained in the dining room floor. A curious sight, the style looked like a small dress shoe and oddly enough, more of a man's design, than a woman's.

Side by side, the two sets demonstrated a moderate stride, originating a couple of feet from the living room, traipsing into the dining room, towards the door, and then vanished. There was nothing on the landing in front of the door – nothing on the stairs; just two simple sets of shoe prints leaving the apartment. I remember how out of place they appeared.

I also wasted no time decorating the apartment, hoping that it would provide a sense of comfort and warmth. I was quick to unpack a lovely wall decoration that my mother had given Jim and I as a wedding gift; a wood sculpture of flowers entwined with vine and leaf. I recall that it was perfect for the fairly large, east wall in the dining room.

With all of our belongings moved into the flat, I remember leaving the windows open all afternoon to see if I could get rid of the haze. Oddly enough, Jim did make a comment, stating that he had noticed it, too. He had remarked that the fog seemed to hang in the room, considering my attempt to air it out. It was very, very strange.

Later that evening, while getting ready for bed, I also recall Jim asking my opinion as to the possible cause of the haze. To me, this indicated that his curiosity had piqued relative to my psychic senses. I responded by telling him that I thought there was some type of existing energy in the room that may be trying to manifest, and that it would probably surface in time. I also told him that I had never come across its *type*, in the past.

A bit temperamental about my response, I reminded him that *he* had advocated the move into the house. He admitted that I did have a point.

Our chat did not make either one of us feel any better, but having lived together for over two years, he knew me well enough to accept that I was more than likely correct. I also remember telling him something to the effect that I had felt that the energy was playing a waiting game. I informed him that I had some type of 'block' going on, and that I could not specifically distinguish its origin. I did, however, state that my gut told me it was more than likely negative.

Another problem that surfaced after the move was the fact that our beloved cat Pooh, would hide and try to escape from the flat, which was something that he had never done before. He also avoided the living room at all costs, which Jim even considered to be unusual.

Pooh simply did not want to be in the front room. Whenever we tried to carry him into it, he would spit, flail and growl, and eventually catapult himself out of our arms, scampering towards our bedroom, or the back of the house. His outlandish behavior demonstrated more than just a cat annoyed by a change of residence.

I recall slight relief, as we approached the end of the first week in the new flat. I had been nightmare-free since the move. I seemed to be sleeping pretty well and the absence of the disturbing dreams came as a blessing – up until a night or so, just before our one-week move-in anniversary. What unfolded in the wee hours of that morning caused me great concern.

As with the dream sequence prior, it began with my being alone and pregnant while searching for my husband, to being driven around in the night, as he turned into a crazed monster as I screamed and begged for him to let me out of the car. Cause remaining unknown, the visions took yet another portentous turn.

During the dream, I had transitioned from being pregnant, to cradling my infant child in my arms. I vaguely remember trying to wake myself up when all of a sudden, the monster stopped the car, and tried to *consume* my baby and I.

I remember trying to protect my newborn as 'it' positioned itself closer to us, while I yelled for help at the top of my lungs. I also remember saying the Lord's Prayer, very loudly in the dream. While reciting the prayer, I recall a brilliant, golden light surround my child, and I.

The last part of the dream was that of me, sitting on the ground protecting my baby, watching the car speed away – and then exploding into the night. As soon as the car had burst into flames, Jim woke me in a panic, with tears in his eyes.

Instinctually, I grabbed my stomach to make sure that I was still pregnant. Becoming aware of my surroundings, I could feel contractions coming along quite strong, every four to five minutes. Once he assured me that I was dreaming, Jim called my mother but she did not answer the phone. He then called his mother, who suggested that we wait and see if the contractions would stop.

While Jim timed the contractions once more, I picked up my Bible and silently read passages to rid the horrible feeling that lingered after the dream had ended. I knew that I had to do something to combat the feeling of doom that the dream had signified.

Disturbed that I had taken the Bible and was sitting in the living room reading it, Jim approached me with quite a brazen attitude. He told me that there was no need for me to be so dramatic, and had insisted that I put it away and get back to bed. I was slightly surprised with his behavior, but given the tiring and frightening ordeal, he had every right to be ornery. Still, his usual comforting demeanor was replaced by a rather nasty and uncalled for, disposition.

As time would tell, neither of us went back to bed. The contractions came as close as three minutes apart, and off to the hospital we went. After admission for 24-hour observation, and having explained to my Obstetrician that I woke up from a terrifying dream contracting, he assured me that there was nothing for me to be concerned about. I never did tell him that it was a very bizarre series of nightmares, but I have little doubt it would have made a difference.

I remember that I was extremely fatigued upon returning to the apartment. I also recall my surprise upon opening the door to the flat, and finding my cherished wood and floral sculpture on the dining room floor: It had broken into two pieces! Encouraging me that a little bit of glue would do the trick, Jim took to the project as I rested, trying to figure out how it had fallen down.

Later, I disclosed greater details of the dreams to Jim, in which case he told me that he would never do anything to hurt the baby, or I. Once again, he resorted back to the 'pepper and cheese' analogy as a means to distract me from worry. Over and done with, Jim said that it was time to move forward and stop thinking about the horrible visions.

* * * * * * *

As the summer months commenced, so did the traditional Fourth of July parties. Most noticeably, my dreams had come to a complete standstill and stopped after the last, but something completely unforeseen began to take place that added to my sense of uneasiness about the flat.

During one of the Fourth of July celebrations, Jim began to drink heavily. Surrounded by friends while at a party next door, he and a couple of his buddies overindulged to the point that one of them stayed at Len and Sarah's, while our friend Chris, came over and slept on our living room couch.

What a fiasco! Trying to situate one drunken man into bed is difficult enough, but on this night, I was trying to care for two, and was eight months pregnant to-boot!

After helping Jim to bed, I then focused on preparing Chris' guest bed on the couch. Luckily, Chris could have cared less about what type of blanket or pillow he had; he was just happy to be able to crash in a safe place, without having to drive. Shortly thereafter, they both passed out. Aside from hearing an occasional wretch into the garbage pail during the early morning hours, Chris and Jim slept rather well – or so, I had thought.

There is nothing more pitiful (yet slightly amusing) than seeing two men wake up with hangovers. I prepared a small breakfast for them and sat at the table, listening to both of them swear that they would never drink again. Chris was never a big drinker to begin with, so I was more apt to buy into his denouncement of all things booze, but I was not too sure about Jim. I recall that it was shortly after their discussion about drinking, when Chris mentioned having a "wild dream."

Referencing the night prior, Chris asked Jim what he had given him to drink. Evidently, Jim was playing bartender and had stirred up a few mystery concoctions. Not blaming it on a specific ingredient, Chris elaborated on his dream, stating that it was like having "a dream, of a dream."

Continuing with the details, he stated that in the dream, he was asleep on our couch, when a man came to his side. The man told him to get up, and go open the door. Chris got up off of the couch and walked in the direction that the man had showed him. Upon arriving at the door, Chris opened it, but almost fell out of the *living room window.* He said that upon waking up from the dream, he half expected to be standing on the window ledge, looking onto 19th Street!

Blaming a night of hard liquor as the culprit, the two friends barely finished their breakfast and parted ways. Of course they both found Chris' dream recollection entertaining; however, I did not find it the least bit comical. As a matter of fact, I was somewhat alarmed. Noting my concern, Jim told me not to read into it, and ended the conversation.

A day or two later, while during a different Fourth of July party that was held at a local park, I had grown miserable from the day's heat and had asked to be taken home. To my knowledge, Jim had not been drinking, and swore that he was sober. I had not seen him raise a beer, or anything other than water to his lips, the entire afternoon. We left on the premise that he would drop me off and return to the party without me: I just wanted to get out of the heat and lay down.

On the way home, I remember Jim was swerving the car. Bringing this to his attention, he became very defensive and began to drive more erratically. Trying to maintain composure, I began to plead with him to pull over. That was when his expression changed to one I would describe as intent to harm. That expression specifically resulted in a flashback to my terrible dreams, and the maniacal fiend that had taken control of the vehicle.

I remember closing my eyes and praying that he would pull over and let me drive, but he was hell-bent on trying to scare me, all the while gaining speed. I do not remember exactly what caused the crash, because my eyes were closed, but I do remember what he said, just before I heard a loud bang, and felt us being thrust backwards, and off the shoulder of the road.

"Oh God, this is it!" I remember yelling. The next thing that I recall was as an eerie silence interrupted by the hissing sound of a leaking radiator. I did not know if Jim was injured or had been killed, until I looked over and saw him sitting at the wheel smiling, as if nothing happened.

The driver of the other car had immediately gotten out and began to yell at Jim. Noticing I was pregnant, the middle-aged man asked if I needed help.

Somewhat sore, and more frightened than anything else, I told him that I was fine. I can recall the strange look on Jim's face as he sat in the driver's seat, not saying a word. I remember questioning him as to why he was smirking. *Was he losing his mind?*

Within minutes, the police arrived. One Officer spoke to Jim, while another spoke to the driver of the other vehicle, who I could clearly hear blaming Jim for the accident, and rightfully so. I also remember the man stating he had crossed the median.

Within minutes, an ambulance arrived and checked everyone to make sure that we were not injured. Considering what could have happened, we were all blessed to be alive.

An Officer then questioned me about the accident. I stated that Jim was taking me home from a party. Jim had told me that he had not been drinking, but it was apparent that he was under the influence of something because he was unable to safely operate the car.

I also stated that I was upset and had asked Jim to let me drive, but he refused, growing unstable. He then asked me what

I remembered about the accident: I informed him that I had closed my eyes, just before the impact.

I then told the Officer what my husband had stated just prior to hearing the crash – even the Police Officer couldn't believe it! He turned to Jim and asked, "Did you tell your wife you were going to *kill* her?"

Although Jim replied with a "No," the grin on his face, in combination with his demeanor, said it all. He looked as though he was *enjoying* the fiasco, and had no remorse.

Jim was arrested after failing a sobriety test, and a short while later, the Officers took me home to the flat. The car had to be towed for repair.

Taking his bizarre behavior into account, I questioned if Jim was having a mental health issue. Surely before that day, he had never acted like that, nor made such a proclamation. One moment he loved me, and was the most wonderful husband on the planet, and the next, he was driving down the middle of the road telling me that he was going to kill me. *What was going on?*

For obvious reasons, Jim's ticket resulted in him losing his license. He did apply for a conditional license in order to drive to, and from work. In the back of my mind I had a feeling that he was not going to respect the law, or the associated terms and conditions of his license. I also made a promise to never get into the car with him as a driver, until he proved that he was responsible, even once he had his license back.

After that ordeal, he would later tell me that he thought the whole situation was funny, and that he was only trying to scare me. I remember reminding him that it was not the least bit amusing; he could have killed us all, inclusive of the baby, *and* the driver of the other car.

Following the car's repair, Jim's operation of the vehicle was restricted, as anticipated. He did not like the fact that I had to chauffer him around and constantly complained about his lack of freedom.

It became evident that his moods would worsen when we were at home. I could not identify an actual trigger that would cause the change; we truly did not argue that often at all. The only thing that I noted was the irritating feeling that blanketed the flat. It rubbed us both the wrong way, and we frequently seemed to be on-edge.

By mid-July, I developed Pre-eclampsia: An extremely dangerous condition that causes large amounts of protein in the urine during pregnancy, which can lead to uncontrolled hypertension. Untreated, it can lead to stroke and death of the mother – and the baby, as well.

Admitted into the hospital for just about one week, my condition stabilized and I was put on bed rest. That in its self, proved to be a daunting task.

We did have some great news, which came during my hospitalization: The Sonogram Technician informed us that we were going to have a girl! Having narrowed baby names down to one for each sex, we were delighted to tell everyone about Leah Michelle!

Responding to treatment, I managed to get through that scare without complication, but found myself not feeling well again, come early August. Approaching my due-date, I had gone from doing great, to feeling pretty awful.

Considering the summer heat, and given the fact that I was in my last month of pregnancy, I found some relief by going out for late-night walks with Sarah, and her sister, Becky. Sadly, Jim had resumed his binge drinking and during nights out, I would leave the oppressive flat and visit Sarah, staying at her house as late as I could to avoid the very unusual feeling that seemed to be intensifying in the house.

I did not like being there at all, let alone having to stay by myself. I began to feel as though I was not welcome in my own home, due to the strange vibe that shrouded 207.

The atmosphere in the living room was very negative and further added to my total state of discomfort. I look back and can still remember that the energy was obscure, but seemed to dislike me, in particular.

After waking alone one night to the sounds of a loud crash, I remember lying in bed, trying to gather my wits; I had no idea what happened, other than I was certain something had fallen in the dining room. Eventually gathering the nerve to scope things out, I found my beloved floral wall sculpture had once more plummeted to the floor. Oddly, it did not break in the areas Jim had previously repaired, but did so in a different section. Putting the pieces onto the table, I walked over to the wall, placing my hand against it to feel for any type of vibration that may have triggered it loose: Nothing.

Letting it dry for well over a week, I decided to move the sculpture to the north wall of the room, switching it with another piece of artwork. Slightly heavier than the large picture, I could not understand why the floral piece was affected, but not the lithograph. Surely, it was not going to survive too many more falls.

During this time, I also spent quite a few nights at my grandmother, Meme's. Not only was it a relief from having to stay at 207, it was great to spend some time with her. Always welcoming me with open arms, I was at peace when I stayed there; that lurking and unsettling feeling seemed to melt away, like a distant distraction.

My due-date of August 21st came – and then passed – without event. Advised by my doctor that this was normal for a first-born, all that it meant for me was prolonged misery. By then, I remember feeling as though I had been pregnant for an entire year.

The late night walks continued, as did Jim's partying, but there was something different about him that I could not quite put my finger on. His actions were slightly 'off,' even when sober. He seemed fine when we were at his parents, or with our friends, but within the privacy of our home, he was becoming controlling and borderline obsessive about what I was doing.

Thinking that perhaps Jim was anxious about the arrival of Leah, I tried to disregard his moods. All the while, the atmosphere of the flat grew more tyrannical in nature.

No sooner had we survived being killed in the car accident, when another scare occurred, while boating on the Mohawk River with some of our friends and my in-laws. What had started as a day of relaxation on the water, narrowly avoided having ended in tragedy.

Known to enjoy the sport of tubing, our friend's children were having a blast that day, as their father whipped them around the river on their inflatable donuts. Typical August weather for Upstate New York, it was hot, yet overcast, but nonetheless provided excellent conditions for boating and water sports.

While our friend had spent the better part of the day captaining his boat, Jim had been drinking, while my mother-in-law sat quietly, keeping a nervous eye on everyone, including a very pregnant me. I remember the gentle motion of the boat had a soothing affect on my condition.

Normally, Jim had always been very careful about protecting me from any type of injury, albeit for the car incident a few weeks prior, but on this particular day, he thought it would be great fun to take over navigating the boat, to create a series of waves as a means of inducing my labor. Needless to say, I was not the least bit enthused with such a dangerous idea.

Astonished that he obliged, our friend relinquished the helm, and with both my mother-in-law and I begging for Jim to stop, he began to wildly zigzag across the river while whipping the kids back and forth on the tubes. With each pass underneath the bridge, he grew progressively more daring with his stunts. Amused at first, Jim's actions quickly had upset our friend.

Laughing like a crazed man, my husband was completely out of control! From what I remember, it was close to twenty minutes that he continued to swing the boat around, creating new sets of breakers, gunning the boat, and bouncing the vessel over them. As our friend tried to carefully regain control of the boat, and with everyone else holding on for dear life, my mother-in-law was on the verge of a mental breakdown from the stress of the situation.

Hysterically laughing, he would circle around and repeat the actions. It was awful. I remember experiencing lower back pain and becoming very worried that I was going to go into labor on the boat. I was also concerned the boat was going to flip over, or the kids were going to get hurt; God forbid, even both.

It was as though Jim had completely disconnected from reality and was unaware of what harm he was causing: He thought it was rip-roaring funny that we were scared. Our friend realized that enough was enough, and finally regained control of the boat. After a long day on the water, we pulled the boat back into the marina. One can only imagine how grateful we were to have made it safely back to shore, without incident, or accident.

Jim had passed-out in the front seat of the car as I drove my in-laws home. During the brief trip back to Troy, my mother-in-law expressed her concern. She had remarked that Jim was not acting right – even if he had been drinking. I couldn't have agreed with her more.

Something was different about my husband: I could see it, as could others. At times he was completely doting and respectful, while at others, even sober, he would turn into a split personality to the likings of Dr. Jekyll, and Mr. Hyde. More disturbing was the fact that on occasion, he could not remember what he was doing.

Interrupting his nap upon arrival at my in-laws, he had absolutely no recollection of the treacherous scene that he had created on the Mohawk. I believed this to be true based upon his somber demeanor. Concerned, my husband stated that he most always remembered things, but admitted that he was having an especially hard time as of late, recalling certain events.

I did begin to wonder if he was involved with heavy-duty drugs. Something was affecting his moods and memory, happening both while sober, and while under the influence of alcohol. I reminded him that alcohol was not an excuse, but it was a factor, and his inability to recall his behavior more so while sober, was extremely concerning. Irritated, and acknowledging the facts, my husband did not think it was anything worth worrying over.

* * * * * * *

34

During the first week in September, I had developed a fever and was put on antibiotics for a kidney infection. Two weeks overdue, I could not imagine how much longer I was going to have to carry little Leah. I also began to question why a doctor would wait so long, even if she were my first child.

Barely able to stand due to a high temperature, I knew something had to be done and called my physician, who advised me to meet him at the hospital. I was terribly sick.

My husband left work to accompany me. As ill as I was, I had no choice but to drive. Advised that I would more than likely be induced, Jim and I fetched the "go bag," and headed to Albany.

Tests revealed that I still had a kidney infection, was extremely dehydrated, and seriously over-due. A new ultrasound also had revealed that I had barely an ounce of amniotic fluid surrounding Leah. I was in danger of losing my baby without prompt care.

Even more startling was the fact that Leah was not a girl. After asking what we were going to name "him," the hospital Sonogram Technician noticed the stunned looks on our faces. Telling her that we were under the impression that Leah was a girl, she confirmed that we were actually having a baby boy! Oops!

One comical moment that I have shared with my son, has to do when Jim realized that my entire "go bag" was full of pink clothing. Ecstatic that he was going to have a son, he wanted to make sure Jimmy Jr. would not be leaving the hospital dressed in pink. Horrified at the thought, he pulled out each item, inspecting the girly clothing, while shaking his head in disbelief. I don't think that it took him two minutes to start making phone calls, advising everyone of the news, and asking them to buy some "boy clothes" for Jimmy.

Due to my mother living rather far away, she could not be at the hospital when I was induced the next morning. As it would be, I was thankful to have my best friend Carol, present at the time. After work, she came to help me with my laboring. That came as much-needed comfort, given Jim had managed to get himself kicked out of my room for becoming unjustifiably argumentative and impatient.

On September 15th, 1988, after 36 hours of pure, tailbone-breaking back labor, Jimmy was born via Cesarean Section. What an exhausting and joyous occasion!

As my doctor later informed us, had I waited another day or two, he probably would have died from aspirating meconium in utero. I felt so incredibly blessed. Jimmy was a healthy, 7-pound, 8-ounce bundle of joy, and Jim was in his glory. It was a welcome change considering he had been extremely irritated just hours before.

Shortly after Jimmy and I came home from the hospital, I took my mother's advice and developed a schedule. I managed to do what I could, even though Jim continued to commemorate his new title of 'father,' by turning it into a weeklong celebration. Once more, Chris had to crash on our couch, as a result of excessive alcohol intake.

Up for an early feeding with Jimmy, I noticed that the living room light had been turned on at some point after Chris had fallen asleep. Heading into the living room, I turned it off and had just about made it back to the dining room, when Chris mumbled something that sent shivers down my spine.

"Don't turn it off," he managed to stammer in a drunken stupor. "That guy wants me to jump out the window."

I immediately concluded that Chris was recounting his former dream. I would inquire more about it in the morning, as he had never left the light on before.

Sure enough, Chris and Jim woke up, and had once again gathered at the dining room table, with their heads hanging low. They were a quiet lot: Neither one of them said much at all. I remember thinking that it was a good time for me to ask Chris if he had any recollection of requesting that I keep the living room light on.

With a look of surprise, he stated that he had another "messed up" dream about the man trying to get him to jump out the living room window. Chris refused to think anything more of it, than an inability to handle his liquor. Careful not to upset the recovering revelers, I decided to call Sarah to see if she had heard Chris mention anything about the first dream. She had not.

Discussing the issue with Jim just met with agitation on his behalf. He did not want to hear anything about it, and said that Chris was right. Senseless to argue about it, the topic was dropped, but I could not help but feel there was something skulking about the front room.

I had found that praying myself to sleep at night was the best way to combat that obtrusive feeling that would not go away. Thankful that my nightmares had completely stopped, I remember that I could not help but wonder why Chris was having his own repetitive terrors.

Having observed that Chris was normally not a heavy drinker, I did ask Jim about his thoughts relative to the recent change. Typically responsible and trouble-free, Jim stated that Chris was a good guy, who had been "partying" a little too hard. He also alluded to the fact that it was probably a stage he was going through.

There were so many noticeable changes with my husband and Chris, as well. I could not help but discount the 'phase' theory, and leaned more towards the influence being that of the house. I also remember that I began to sense that we were living in a vortex more than a portal, due to the presence of at least *two* different energies, and that relentless haze.

* * * * * * *

Sometime in early November, Chris had told Jim that he felt lousy about all of the increased drinking he was doing and informed him that he was going to give up alcohol. He also stated that he was looking to meet a nice girl, more specifically, one of my best friends. Jim had told Chris about Carol, and knowing that Chris was a decent guy, suggested we set up a double date.

Not too long after our conversation, Chris came over to our flat to meet my friend. Seeming to hit it off right away, an official double date was planned for around the holidays.

After their introduction, Carol went home and Chris decided to hang out and visit with Jim. Jim tossed back a few brews that night, and although Chris did not have a single drink, he asked to stay over and sleep on the couch.

It was close to 4:00AM when there arose a terrible commotion in the living that shot Jim out of bed, feet barely touching the floor. My heart raced, unable to discern what the noise was. That was when I heard Jim call out, "What the hell are you doing, man?" It didn't take me too long to get into the living room, where I had found a rather precarious situation unfolding before my very eyes.

Chris was standing at the window, visibly shaken. When asked what had caused the disruption, Chris initially told my husband that he did not want to talk about. He looked like he was in shock.

Whether to be a wise-ass, or to break the mood, Jim poked fun at Chris and asked if "the dream man" had spooked him. Chris was not pleased by Jim's insensitivity given the situation – and neither was I. I recall Chris becoming quite upset with Jim's remark, and having what I would describe, as a mini-meltdown. I did not know what to think.

Unhappy that Jim was making fun of his friend, I could not help but wonder why he was being so callous with Chris, given his emotional state: He was cruel. Jim was way out of line.

It was as though he was amused that his pal was scared to death. Jim's changeable moods were like watching a hidden alter ego emerge, wreak havoc, and then retreat – and there was no way to tell when it would surface. I hated to see him humiliate Chris, and remember asking him to knock it off.

Chris then sat on the couch and asked me to take him home. Sitting by his side, I tried to figure out what had happened when he began to describe what he thought had caused the noise:

At some point in his dream, he stated that he was *yanked* off of the couch and thrown towards the window by the same man he had seen in the dreams before. Petrified during the dream, he woke up and realized that he was literally standing at our living room window, with his hands on the glass. *Whoa!* I can tell you that even today, just the thought of what he said that morning, still makes me shudder – the whole night does.

Having practiced 'blocking' since day one of going to see 207, it dawned on me that the menacing feeling that enveloped the flat could possibly be the man in Chris' dreams. I sensed that there was some type of association between the two, which was lending clues through *both* of our outlandish visions.

Given my grandmother's advice, I knew enough not to "call *it* out." I remember thinking that I would just have to wait, and will be forever thankful that it was something I knew enough to avoid.

As I drove Chris home, I remember that he was very quiet. After extending an apology for scaring me, in addition to asking me to drive him home, the only other thing that he stated, was that he would never sleep on our couch again. He also stated that he did not like the flat. Questioning what to do about the upcoming date with Carol, he said that he would meet us out – he didn't even want to hang out at the house any more.

In all honesty, I was not up for another fright-fest, if he had slept over. I could tell he was troubled and trying to process what had happened, but was hoping that he would say something – anything – that would provide more evidence as to the source of the problem.

All that I knew, was it was his third nightmare while sleeping on our sofa. The only piece of information that I had was a non-descript male had been coming to him during the dream, and was trying to get him to jump out the window. Vague, the message was still quite ominous.

That following morning, I called my maternal grandmother Marie, to ask her advice about Chris' unusual dreams. I recall the hesitation in her voice, as she explained that sometimes Fallen Angels become attached to particular places, people, and even items, and create experiences similar to what we had been having, in varying degrees. Reassuring me that I would be fine so long as I asked for protection, she suggested that I consider asking Father to come over and do a house blessing at 207.

The next night, all hell broke loose when I proposed that very idea to Jim. Never before had I seen him become so enraged. As a matter of fact, up to that point, I can say with certainty that I had only seen him that angry maybe once, during the entire time we had been together, not counting that the day of the car accident.

Confused as to his reaction, I remember thinking how silly it all seemed for him to respond so radically, when all I did was express my concern. He had always advocated Father to be part of our lives. Why was it such a problem to have him do a blessing?

Troubled by my husband's response, I found no harm in having our priest bless the flat. Father was an open-minded man. He had married us, tried to counsel us after my miscarriage, and at the time, was about to baptize Jimmy: No matter how many times I would ask, Jim vehemently protested.

Frustrated, I remember begging him to give me valid grounds to support his disdain. The only reason he would share with me, was that he felt no need to have Father come and go through a blessing, since Chris was not going to come back to sleep on the couch. Bringing up the strange coincidence of my nightmares, in addition to Chris', he argued that since mine had stopped, it simply did not matter.

After a very heated argument, Jim stormed off. The tension in the air was horrible.

Later than night, while in the front room, I remember turning off the television and sitting in the quiet; Jimmy nestled in the nursery. I inspected every inch of that front room, trying to distinguish the energies and identify what could be going on. They seemed to be changeable, shifting back and forth from one moment to the next. The energies appeared as though they were 'charging' themselves, and would equate the feeling to someone revving the engine of a car, warming up for a big take off. I can still recall how heavy the air was, even with the new wall color and finished floor: The entire room always felt the same, and I did not like it one bit.

During my inspection that night, I had moved the coffee table out of the way, and rolled up the area rug that we had placed in the middle of the room. Gathering my bearings, I remember trying to stand in the same spot that had once been abandoned by the sander.

After several long minutes of analyzing the area, I could not see anything. If something had been there, it had been removed when Jim had refinished the floor. Returning the furniture and rug to its original state, I sat in the chair and scrutinized the space, some more.

Whatever they were, the energies appeared to be growing stronger with each passing day. I knew that I could not be afraid, and was aware that those types of energies thrived on fear. I did, however, want to make it known that they were not welcome in my house.

If my memory serves me correctly, it was just a few days after the house blessing argument, that I had one of the worst nightmares of *my life*. I will never, ever forget it, as long as I live.

With the head of our bed positioned between the two doors that accessed our bedroom from the dining room, my side of the bed was to the left. I also sleep on my right side, which for sake of this description, put my back towards the door on that night.

During the dream, the hand of a *creature* reached from the dining room, around the door, and into the bedroom, trying to grab me from the back of my head. The claw-like hand was covered with a black sleeve, much like that of a robe.

Fearing for my life, I grabbed Jimmy out of his crib and remember screaming the name of the Lord for protection, as the creature chased me through a fiery darkness. Shouting for help, I ran as fast as I could while covering Jimmy, as flames shot up all around us. The creature was relentless, and even though it was faceless, radiated pure evil. Although a short vision, I awoke hyperventilating and praying out loud.

Scared out of my wits, I went to the nursery to check on Jimmy, who was sound asleep. I then proceeded into the living room with my Bible in hand. I recall fumbling through passages, praying as hard as I could: *I was scared to death.* I must have prayed for at least two hours.

I remember that the sun had started to rise, when out of the silence of the breaking dawn, Jim began screaming from his own night terror. My heart about fell out of my body!

After a brief, guttural scream, I walked into the dining room and peeked into the right side of the bedroom, where I saw my husband sitting up, in a daze. Trembling, I noticed that his eyes were cast downward at the floor, as though he was half-asleep.

Within moments of sitting up, he laid back down and closed his eyes, as though nothing had happened. As daylight had started to gleam through the sides of the window shades, I was too startled to go back to bed.

Returning to the chair in the living room, I opened the Bible once more and randomly turned to Psalm 11, and began to read it aloud, every so softly. I knew that the lurid dream was a premonition, and ended the Psalm by praying, *"Dear God, please help us."*

4

Phantom Odor

Having had abilities most of my life, I had learned to rely on my maternal grandmother Marie, for advice on paranormal issues. Even long before paranormal investigations existed in the way they do today, she had told me to scrutinize the situation, to see if it was something truly paranormal taking place, or not. She also told me to always ask for God's guidance.

Over time, friends and acquaintances would contact me, stating that they thought their homes, or apartments, were haunted. Taking notes, I would go to their residences, ask a host of questions, and then read the energy fields to determine if I could pick up on anything unusual. Some of them would turn out to be experiencing paranormal activity while a larger number of others, were not.

Long before fancy ghost hunting equipment came along, I learned to rely solely on my instincts and abilities, which strengthened with each new experience. If a property appeared to be haunted, I would say a prayer and conduct either a holy water blessing, or a sea salt-water blessing. Although my grandmother had instructed me on how to do a sage smudging, up until my late twenties, I had only conducted one while visiting with her several years prior.

Regardless, up until moving into 207, most of my 'cases' were simple and harmless energies that were more of a nuisance to the residents. Having heard of darker energies and Fallen Angels, I certainly had not encountered one beforehand, which equated to rather limited experience by the time that I had turned twenty-three, and moved into the flat. With time, however, I learned to discern the different characteristics of negative and positive energies, with and without spirit activity.

Perhaps the most complicated issue that I had ever run into was a stubborn spirit who inhabited an older home and did not want to leave. Not harmful to its residents, it chose to cross very quickly after guiding it out, and conducting a blessing. Today, that would not have been of any significant challenge, considering what I have experienced since those times.

* * * * * * *

Concerned about the very unfamiliar feeling that permeated every nook and cranny of 207, more so in the front living room, I tried to locate reading materials to help me identify the energies that were steadily demolishing my home. Sometimes the energies seemed incredibly strong, while at other times, they appeared to be on standby.

The only other thing that I could sense was that it felt more male-oriented at times. Considering the details of Chris' dreams, I was pretty certain this was the case, but I was unable to actually 'read' it. It always reverted back to an enigma, of sorts. It also felt very old – almost ancient, in nature.

In my opinion, although I could not seem to 'see' any other details, I knew that there was more than one type of energy, due to the shifts, and due to the difference in emotions that the shifts would cause. Several people had commented that they had felt uncomfortable in 207, yet could not specifically state why. Often, these sentiments occurred without any type of provocation.

Having questioned Jim's wild mood swings and behavioral changes, and given what odd feelings took float around the flat, I knew that I was in need of more guidance. I do remember briefly considering if I should contact a Psychic, but did not know if that was the right approach to take. I also did not think that anyone would be interested in coming to the flat to investigate. I recall feeling somewhat helpless; I was doing the best that I could, to protect my family with prayer.

When I had contacted my grandmother, she reminded me (as she so often did), never to use a Ouija Board, or anything of its sort, in the house. I didn't argue with her about that, as she had shared a very frightening story with me, and had cemented in my brain, how dangerous they were. She then suggested a house blessing by sage smudging, but I was concerned about Jimmy being around the smoke from the ceremony. My grandmother also recommended that I could use holy water, adding that my husband should be part of the blessing, as to protect the whole family.

I knew that asking Jim to take part in a house blessing was going to be a tough sell, especially since he had emphatically told me that he did not want our priest to do one. I remember thinking that I could at least suggest it, but was quite wary about doing so.

My grandmother also told me that she would try to 'read' the flat, to see if anything would come up. As with both of our abilities, many times energies and spirits will present themselves during dreams. I completely understood her reasoning to wait a few days, as that was something that I had been accustomed to myself, when deciphering energies.

Of Roman Catholic faith, my grandmother strongly believed that having Father do the blessing was the best-case scenario, but also knew that it was not worth pushing Jim's buttons. She also stated that I should go ahead and conduct one on my own, as in her opinion, it was better to be safe, than sorry. Wishing me the best, and surrounding me with light and prayer, she said that she would call back in a few days and let me know if anything came through on her end.

Later that day, while conversing with Jim over dinner, I mentioned my grandmother's suggestion about doing a blessing without Father. He lost his temper and things got ugly.

He completely went bananas, yelling that under no circumstances was I, or anyone else, to do a blessing in the house, citing that they – house blessings – were a "bunch of bullshit." Trying to get him to better understand how I felt, was useless. Telling me that I was not to mention the subject again, I was also warned not to breathe a word about it to Father at Jimmy's baptism, which was scheduled for the end of November.

My options seemed to dwindle. I struggled to please him, and tried to avoid agitating him. I never knew what would set him off; it was like walking on eggshells.

Knowing that I had to try and take control of my home, I decided to take matters into my own hands by conducting a house blessing using holy water, the next day while Jim was at work. There would be no way for him to tell.

* * * * * * *

It was a beautiful day for a blessing. Although it was chilly, I was able to open all of the apartment windows to ensure the energies a swift exit.

Taking the holy water, I blessed myself and Jimmy, placing him in his playpen with a few toys to keep him busy in the dining room while I blessed the flat. I then made the sign of the cross, and recited a Catholic prayer at the front entrance to the apartment. I also asked God to protect my family and I, as we came in to, and left our home. I also asked all of those who entered, to know God's peace, and love.

I next proceeded into the kitchen, followed by the dining room, the bedrooms, and the bathroom and lastly the living room, reciting a specific prayer for each. When finished, I returned to the front door of the flat, where I *insisted* that whatever evil was present in 207 leave, as it was not welcome in our Christian home. Reciting a final prayer, I blessed myself and Jimmy one more time, and concluded the ceremony.

In a matter of less than twenty minutes, it was done. I felt somewhat at peace knowing that I did it without angering my husband.

In the meantime, I was eager to see if the haze dissipated, or the energy shifts stopped. I also had to wait and hear back from my grandmother, as to whether or not she was able to pick up on anything.

It only took a day before my grandmother called me back. From the moment she spoke her first words, I could tell that she was worried. In an attempt to make me feel better, she told me that nothing specific came through, but wanted to know the next time I would be visiting our priest. That was an easy answer, as Jimmy was going to be baptized within the upcoming week.

Unable to make the long trip down for Jimmy's celebration, she urged me to talk to Father about what was going on. Advising her that I blessed the flat with holy water, she insisted that it was still important that I spoke with him about the events.

When I asked her what she thought was going on at 207, I remember that she would only tell me that she felt it had something to do with a church. *A church?* That threw me for a loop.

Saint Patrick's Roman Catholic Church was *very* close by, with a handful of smaller churches scattered throughout the city. Asking her for more details, she would only state that she was unsure, but did feel the energies were somehow connected to a church.

I could tell that she was exercising caution, relative to what she told me. I also recall thinking that she probably did not want to scare me, which in my opinion meant that she had picked up on something significantly unpleasant. I had a sneaking suspicion that my grandmother had probably sensed something that was too far over my head, to explain.

I remember feeling like I was in between a rock, and a hard

place: If I talked to Father it would be construed as an act of betrayal, which would infuriate my husband. The more thought that I gave the situation, even considering my grandmother's advice, the more I knew that I would just have to wait and see what would happen, since I had recently conducted the house blessing.

A few more days passed, and there did not appear to be any change in the heavy feeling that hung in the air, yet everything else remained peaceful. Plans were implemented for Jimmy's baptism, and we were all looking forward to his big day.

It was within days just prior to the baptism, that I dropped Jim off at work and spent most of the afternoon at my mother-in-law's, making plans for the celebration. Later, I had picked Jim up from work and headed home to the flat.

Halfway up the stairs, we both began to smell something very foul. Not overtly a sulfur smell, it was more of a mixture of different pungent odors. The closer we got to the door, the stronger it became – and that worried us. We both thought there was a problem with one of the gas pipes, but based upon further examination of the scent, were leaning more towards an animal having died inside one of the walls.

Opening the door to the flat was like walking straight into a wall of the most putrid odor imaginable. It was *horrible!*

Without hesitation, Jim checked the gas piping but did not see, or hear anything. The heating unit had not been tampered with, so he began inspecting the other rooms while I took Jimmy downstairs, and stood in the hallway, leaving the front door open. Unable to identify the source, we knew that we had to call Niagra Mohawk, to come and assess the situation.

Due to the severity of the odor, they responded quickly. At first guess, the utility worker stated that it was probably a leaking valve in the furnace system, but also noted that it was not clearly identifiable. He too, seemed a bit confused as to the culprit, and mentioned a dead animal.

After accessing the basement in addition to the other flats, he remained uncertain and advised us that he did not find any obvious cause. He then telephoned his supervisor. The decision was then made to 'tag' the furnace and in turn, instruct everyone to leave the premises. The only thing that he could conclude upon initial investigation, was that the odor was concentrated in the middle of the house – in our flat.

Hastily packing a few items, we left 207, having been advised that Niagra Mohawk would be conducting more tests over the following day and would be in contact with us. The three of us returned to my in-laws, detailing what had happened.

We did not hear back from the power company until two days later. They explained the 'tag' had been removed and that they never found a cause. Additionally, our Landlord advised us that he had gone to 207, to make sure that the odor had completely dissipated, and that it was safe for all Tenants to return.

Not only were Jim and I concerned, but his parents were as well. How could they *not* have found a cause to such a stench, and why was it concentrated in our flat?

Niagra Mohawk insisted that it was safe to return and gave us instructions to call back if we were to notice the odor in the future. Fortunately, that was the lone incident; we never noticed the rotting smell again, and not a hint of it remained.

That Sunday, Jimmy had a wonderful baptismal ceremony surrounded by family and friends. The weather held up and he didn't fuss, one bit. In spite of the fact that it was a perfect day, I was bothered by my husband's lack of enthusiasm.

Always having taken a liking to large gatherings, I recall thinking how strange Jim had behaved. It was almost as though he was lost in private thought. He certainly had not been in a good mood on the way to the baptism, nor after getting back home. He was cordial, but distant during the festivities, and was *very* quiet at home.

* * * * * * *

As Jimmy's first Christmas approached, life in the flat with the exception of the decaying odor, remained uneventful. Most thoughts and tasks were focused on shopping for gifts and making the traditional holiday cookies from my grandmother Marie's, scrumptious family recipes.

Come Christmas Eve, it was quite exciting to decorate a tree for Jimmy. He was going to turn 3-months-old just before the holiday, and had already developed an affection for Kermit The Frog. I fondly recall Jim's nickname for the holiday that year as the "Muppet Christmas."

Putting up the tree was somewhat uneventful – well for the most part. Our choices were to the left, or to the right of the fireplace. Wanting to display the tree in front of the window, I picked the right corner.

Taking a couple of hours to decorate our 6' tall, artificial Blue Spruce, I tucked Jimmy into his crib, and then sat on the couch with Jim to appreciate our masterpiece; it was perfection! However, having to recall what followed our tree-trimming extravaganza still bothers me, almost twenty-three years later.

I remember coming out of the kitchen with a cup of tea and heading into the front room, when I began to pick up on an energy standing in the corner, right in front of the tree. It was the first time that I had actually been able to sense a *specific* presence. I remember that it was very dark and heavy – it was an older male, in black. I could feel steely, cold eyes and a vicious, masochistic arrogance. Taking great care, not to become outwardly excited, or fearful, I walked over to the couch and observed the room's atmosphere, not saying a word about it to my husband. In the relatively short duration of time that it took me to walk from the front room to the kitchen and back, the air had become dense, and warm.

Noticing a change in my mood, Jim had asked what my problem was. No sooner did he finish asking me, did the energy vanish – the feeling was *gone*.

My response was that I had wished we had put the tree in the opposite corner. I stated this due to the manner by which the energy had showed itself. Menacing for certain, my senses told me that it had manifested as a warning. I was incensed that it dared to make itself 'psychically visible' to me on Christmas

Eve, in front of our beautiful tree. The last thing that needed to take place was for Jim to hear me complaining about picking up on the spirit of an evil, dead man, so I left it at that.

I decided that whatever, and wherever the energy was from, it was NOT going to ruin our Christmas – and it was not going to hang out in my home. From the very moment it revealed itself, I had a newfound awareness that it was malevolent, and I remember being greatly troubled by the fact the house blessing had not worked. I was also going to have to be especially attentive to the fact that I had to protect my family. It was making a stand; trying to show me who was boss. I was determined to succeed for if anything, I was not going to let its spawning of fear, control *anyone*.

Jimmy's first Christmas was beautiful, but Jim remained somewhat reserved throughout the day's festivities. Understanding that having a house full of company can make even the best disposition of people cranky, I took it in stride and managed to enjoy the day, cognizant of the showing of the male spirit.

During the late afternoon, we had received a call from one of my husband's cousins, and decided to get out and take a trip to see them after our guests had left. A forty-five minute drive on Christmas Day in good weather was doable, especially when everyone wanted to meet baby Jimmy. It was also a perfect opportunity to get out of the flat.

Jim seemed to be in much better spirits upon arrival at his cousin's house that evening, and although he had a few drinks, I was more than relieved that he did not over-do it. In fact, it was a very pleasant way to end Christmas 1988, nevertheless considering what had been taking place at 207.

5

Push

One of the first tasks to tackle for the new-year was the double date that Jim and I had arranged between Chris and Carol. New beginnings, be it in general or specific to relationships, was something positive. I for one was looking forward to just that: A positive, fresh start.

Since Chris had previously stated that he did not want to go to the house due to his last episode, we had made alternative arrangements. The last thing that I had to do, was to make sure that I could find Jimmy a babysitter for a few hours on the night of the date.

Since Carol had mentioned her plans to her sister (my other best friend), Karen readily volunteered to care for Jimmy while on break, and was looking forward to some quality bonding time with her favorite "bambino." Finalizing our plans, Carol would drive Karen to 207, and after familiarizing Karen with Jimmy's routine, we would go about our merry way.

The night of our double date went without a hitch. Karen was thrilled to help out, and seemed very much at ease. When the three of us left to go pick up Chris, Karen was sitting on the sofa, giving Jimmy his evening bottle. I remember how natural Karen looked cradling Jimmy. She definitely had a strong maternal instinct and I smiled at the thought of her having a clan of her own some day.

We all had a great time at the renowned Holmes & Watson's in downtown Troy. Double dates can be a tad uncomfortable, but Chris and Carol got along very well. I also remember that Jim seemed quite silly that night, which was a welcome change, considering how on and off, he had been leading up then.

Calling it an early night, Carol dropped off Chris at his house first, and then continued onto our flat to fetch Karen. I recall Carol had stayed in the car, and after saying goodnight to Jim and I, asked that we send Karen down, after getting our baby briefing.

Upon unlocking the apartment door, both Jim and I headed towards the living room but did not find Karen present. I also remember that the television was turned off. Thinking that she was probably in the nursery with Jimmy, we turned around and headed in that direction.

Walking through the dining room, I had noticed Karen standing in the kitchen, light on, leaning with her back against the counter; she seemed very nervous, a direct contrast of her demeanor earlier in the evening.

She very quickly filled me in on her time with Jimmy, stating he did well, and that she had enjoyed spending time with him. Telling me that we would chat on the phone in the near future, she headed towards the door somewhat hastily.

Something was up; she was not herself and was rather abrupt on departure. As sweet as always, she gave me a hug and thanked me for letting her come to visit Jimmy, and dashed down the stairs.

Curious as to her obvious change in mood, I began to wonder if perhaps she had fallen asleep on the couch and had a strange dream, like Chris had. It was certainly possible that she may have dozed-off while we were out, but it still would not equate to the fact that she looked *scared*.

Karen was such an intelligent, caring girl. Her keen wit and beautiful personality would light up any room that she walked in to. A little known fact about Karen was that she too, was quite psychic.

Beginning to take note of her abilities, we would have long discussions on the topic, in addition to spirituality. Highly clairvoyant, I knew that whatever paranormal activity she had spoke of, was nothing embellished, or exaggerated.

When things began to unfold at 207, indicating that something other than typical relationship issues were at hand, I had made it a point not to mention anything to her, to see if she would pick up on the energies. This was my motivation for not wanting to immediately tell her, or Carol about the dreams that had taken place.

Knowing that at some point Karen would come over to visit once her schedule permitted, I was curious to see if she could sense anything in the flat. All indications were pointing in that direction, given her behavior when she left that night.

The day after the babysitting adventure, Carol had called me to ask if I had heard from Karen. I told her that I had not, and questioned why. Carol seemed like she wanted to tell me something and then hesitated, telling me that I would best hear it from Karen.

After arousing interest, I remember begging Carol to give me an idea as to what had happened. Carol then stated that Karen had a rather unusual encounter at the apartment, while watching Jimmy. She also said that she was really "freaked out" by the whole thing, and was going to be calling me to discuss what transpired.

Uh oh! If Karen had an experience and Chris had dreams, in addition to some other unusual activities that had been cropping up in the flat, it was definitely not looking very positive.

Later that evening, Karen called. She began by apologizing for her behavior when she had left the house. She then told me about her experience.

The first thing that she had asked me was if I had sensed anything while living there. Hesitating, I told her that I wanted to hear what she had to say first, and would then detail my accounts, as so we could compare notes.

Karen stated that almost immediately after walking into the flat, she picked up on something. She felt like someone was "staring her down." Trying to put it out of mind, she played with Jimmy for a little while after his bottle, and then settled him into the nursery. She then returned to the living room and watched some television.

While watching T.V., she said that she suddenly felt very flushed and became extremely frightened, but could not figure out why. She returned to the nursery to find Jimmy, sleeping soundly in his crib. I recall her voice cracking, as she then explained what happened upon her return to the living room. I could sense the concern in her voice.

According to Karen, she had noticed the television had been turned off. She was certain that it was on when she had gotten up to check on Jimmy. She also said that as soon as she sat in the chair adjacent to the sofa, she felt like someone pushed her downwards, into the chair: She totally lost it.

She stated that for the remaining two hours we were out, she stood in the kitchen, or sat in the rocker in the nursery. She too, had been very frightened. I had no reason to disbelieve Karen, at all. The fact that the energies had become physically aggressive was quite alarming.

On the verge of tears, Karen then told me that as much as she loved Jimmy and I, she could not go back to the flat. She did state that she would watch him again, but it would have to be at someplace other than the apartment.

Concerned, she too, stated that she had never experienced anything violent, as what she did in the flat. I then disclosed what had been occurring since we had moved to Watervliet. Trying to figure out what types of energies were present, the only thing that I could share with her was that one was male. It also seemed as though 'he' was being controlled by another, more potent energy, and together, they were pushing family and friends around – and out of Jim and my lives, as well.

One thing was for sure: Whatever was lurking in the flat was evil. I reminded her that she should not feel ashamed, or bad about refusing to come back to the flat, telling her that Chris said the same thing, but based his feelings on slightly different grounds. With good cause, both Karen and I concluded that someone might have actually died in the house. The questions then remained as to *whom, how, when and why?*

6

Hostile Takeover

As with any marriage or relationship for that matter, Jim and I had our share of disagreements, but for the most part, got along very well. Looking back, Jim's lightheartedness and loyalty, along with his sense of love for family, was what made him so special.

Of German and Irish descent, my husband had a very quick wit and ferocious sense of humor. He was also very in touch with his inner child, and would go full steam ahead when it came time to do anything related to children. Whether dressing up as Santa Claus at Christmastime, or rounding up a handful of kids to take them to the park for the afternoon, Jim was committed to ensuring any child in his care was safe, and able to have fun; something that he did not often experience as a child, himself. Those were truly endearing qualities that strengthened our bond.

I often think back to the story that Carol shared with me, relative to the night Jimmy was born. As mentioned earlier in the book, I had labored long and hard, before having a cesarean section. Given that Jimmy was born just before 1:00AM, it was very late when I had been taken into post-op recovery.

Since Jim was unable to drive, Carol had offered to give him a ride back home to Watervliet. A more than appreciative Jim was walking on air that night, and also in a celebratory mood.

After making sure that I was settled in, the two headed out. It had been a long day for all.

Very soon after Carol and Jim had left the hospital, I began to have the sensation that I was going to the bathroom on my bed sheets. Unsure as to why this was occurring, I was conscious enough to know that I had been catheterized from surgery. I also remember experiencing a rapid onset of dizziness.

Pushing the call light and yelling out for help, my nurse appeared, asking what was wrong. Assessing the situation, she repositioned me, and tried to comfort me by advising that this was fairly normal given the medication and procedure. She then lifted the sheets to make sure they were not wet.

Unfortunately, I will never forget how frightened I became when the nurse her self, began to call for help. I had no idea what was going on.

I can recall a chaotic, flurry of activity. I was extremely woozy and had a difficult time focusing on anything. Listening to the staff's conversation, I could only gather that it was obvious that the dampness that I had felt, along with the sensation of going to the bathroom, was not from urine, but from large amounts of blood, due to hemorrhaging.

My physician was paged to the recovery suite and rattled off a bunch of medication orders. Due to my condition, and given as much as I can remember, he briefly mentioned possibly having to take me back into the operating room if the medications were not successful. I was also in need of a transfusion.

Fortunately, due in part to the quick reaction of the nursing staff and doctor, the combination of medication and transfusion, worked. I slept for most of the remaining night, wondering if anyone had been able to reach Jim to tell him. I also recall worrying about my son.

Considering how late she had left the hospital, Carol was back to work bright and early the next morning. Stopping by to check on me, she mentioned that Jim would be getting a ride to the hospital from a family member, later in the day. She then told me about what happened the night before, on the way home. The big smile on her face said it all.

Apparently, an elated Jim was hooting and hollering out of the car window during their ride yelling, "I'm a father! I have a son!" Jim had also asked Carol to drop him off at his brother's apartment in Troy, in order to continue celebrating. His merriment did not stop there.

Carol stated that Jim then began exclaiming the same sentiments on the front lawn of the apartment complex. She said that she had never seen a man so happy to become a father. It was truly touching for her to see – as well as for me, to hear: That was my Jim.

After Carol told me of the adventure, I explained what had transpired in the recovery room. Everything seemed to have worked out just fine. I was very happy to know that Jim was thrilled, bearing in mind how he had been acting. Jimmy's birth was truly a joyful event, and it was good to know that whatever had been bothering my husband at the time, had been momentarily forgotten with the birth of our son.

* * * * * * *

Once my maternity leave was over, I began a new position working full time at the hospital, in Financial Services. Hoping to return to college at some point in the future, I was strongly considering nursing as a profession, but had an infant son to concentrate on raising first; there was little time for distractions of school at that juncture. Since Sarah had previously offered to care for Jimmy, everything fell into place with one issue remaining at hand: Jim's bizarre behavior continued to skyrocket.

Just shortly after the new-year, my husband took a noticeable turn for the worse. There were times when he would become outright hostile, even when abstemious.

Having a wonderfully supportive mother, and two of the world's best friends, I confided in them relative to the change in my husband's character. I also relied on my grandmother Marie, for moral support. Sadly, aside from the fact that my paternal grandmother and I were very close as well, her health began to deteriorate; her memory was not even close to what it had been and I did not want to confuse, or upset her with those details.

Obviously, my closest confidantes, in addition to some of my work associates, knew of my 'abilities,' but as for everyone else, I had always felt it was best to keep them at bay. During some of our discussions relative to the timeline just prior to, and after moving in to 207, we were in agreement that the flat, or the house, was infested with something dreadful. I wanted to keep things as low-key as possible, and if needed, would have to seek outside help, and call Father...*in private.*

* * * * * * *

Everyone knew that Jim was typically a happy-go-lucky guy, who would do anything to help someone in need. Another great memory that I have shared with our son has to do with the time that I brought Jim lunch, while he was painting the exterior of a large home, in downtown Troy.

Climbing down from the ladder to greet me, he stated that he had too much work to do, and would eat the lunch afterward. Just as we were saying goodbye to one another, a homeless man approached Jim, asking him for change. Not only did Jim give him change, but gave him a twenty dollar bill *and* his lunch, but it was the extra step that he took following that gesture, which made me so proud of him.

Astonished by his generosity, the homeless man graciously thanked Jim, and told him that he would repay him one day. Jim, knowing that he would probably never see the man again, told him not to worry about it, but asked if he would mind answering a few questions.

Jim was very interested in the man's life events which had rendered him to be in such a predicament. He also tried to encourage him, stating that he could turn his life around if he put his mind to it. Jim's compassion was incredible; he was a true Humanitarian.

As I left, the two were deep in the throes of conversation. Once again, Jim managed to fill my heart with great joy, by committing such a random act of kindness. As always, my husband looked out for the underdog.

Today, this trait is evident in our son. Even as a young child, his heart was filled with kindness, so much in fact, that it led to him being honored with his school's "Friendship Award," while in the second grade.

* * * * * * *

Since moving into the flat, Jim's personality had grown progressively more moody, and aggressive. Times of laughter seemed very few and far between.

His erratic mood swings were most perplexing, as I still could not seem to identify their cause. I did, however, notice that he seemed to lighten up whenever we were out of the house, but after spending any considerable time at the flat, he would become highly temperamental, and at times, downright mean.

There were days when we had not even had a disagreement and he would become emotionally volatile. I began to consider that it very well might have had something to do with the hideous male spirit and haunting ambiguous energy, but even at my age, I was still learning about my gifts: I had limited experience on the subject matter.

Usually very confident and outspoken, I found that even my own personality had adjusted to Jim's altered state, and the abrasive atmosphere of the flat. I became quiet and less communicative. For sake of keeping Jim on an even keel, most of our conversations were simplistic. I was especially concerned about his behavior around Jimmy, as he was quick to fly off the handle. I knew that he loved us, but it also appeared that he was falling into a dark, and bottomless pit.

For sake of transparency, and somewhat humiliating to admit, I must mention another change that took place with Jim. Within a month or so, after moving in to the flat, my husband began to obsess over pornography. Prior to moving into 207, he had *occasionally* rented a video, but it had quickly become a ridiculous, and unhealthy fascination.

By early 1989, I began to hear off-handed quips from his friends regarding him owning a "hidden 'flick' collection." Apparently, when I had left for an appointment, or went out on an errand while he was home, he would take them out.

Combing through a few boxes in his closet while he was gone one afternoon, I discovered the existence of some very disturbing adult films. I did confront him with the tapes and told him that it was absolutely unacceptable to watch those types of movies, let alone have a compilation of such lewd material. His concealed collection was far beyond hardcore – and absolutely disgusting. Although they were not illegal (meaning; no child pornography), I did not want him watching them, nor did I want them in my house. I vividly recall him stating that my reaction was amusing, which made the situation even more peculiar.

Imploring he throw them out, he stated that he would get rid of them. Later advised by a friend, I found out that he had given them to someone else for safekeeping, periodically going to their house to view them. I was sickened by the whole situation. That was not normal, by any standards.

Recalling a conversation with a mutual friend, I had asked what they thought of Jim's behavior. Stating that he seemed to be acting like he was "off his rocker" at times, they had noticed quite a few instances where he had become hostile without reason. They also mentioned a situation that occurred during a weekend gathering to watch a football game.

Having known him since childhood, the friend stated that they were actually somewhat shocked by my husband's actions. Jim liked to wager a few dollars in the game's pool, but was not a big gambler. Miffed that he had lost, he intentionally picked a fight with one of his pals, which sparked an even bigger argument. Allegedly, Jim went after his friend and had gotten kicked out of the house. Nodding my head in understanding, I confided that I too, had noticed the random outbursts of violence.

During this time period, my job had become a pleasant distraction. I felt much more at ease at work, knowing that Jimmy and I were out of the house. Regrettably, Jim's moods continued to grow of more concern.

From time to time, I would pick up on the male spirit and came to notice that the secondary force was impacting it much like the actions of a puppet master, to their doll. Acclimated to 'blocking' it upon its presentation, I still could not stand to be around it. It was extremely intimidating, almost exhibiting a profound sense of cruelty.

I cannot recall the exact date, but I had gone to stay with Meme for that very rationale. Thinking that Jim would be gone for the weekend, I packed enough for Jimmy and I to get through one night, and headed over to her apartment for a visit.

I do remember it being a Saturday night, and that I had called Carol to see what plans she had. Unknowing that Jim had recently contacted her inquiring of my whereabouts, she advised him that she had not yet heard from me, and therefore had no idea.

Jim did not believe her and stated the following, "Carol, I have never had a problem with you, and if you want to keep it that way, you *will* tell me where Jill is." He had threatened her.

She insisted that she was telling him the truth, in which she was, and the call ended abruptly. As she would later tell me during our conversation, she was actually "afraid" of him – the modulation of his voice was disturbing. She would also state that she never heard him act, or talk that way, in all of the time she had known him.

By the time that I was able to return Jim's call after Carol had advised me of their conversation, he had already left 207. I stayed put, and spoke with him much later that night.

It was fruitless trying to convince him that I was at my grandmother's for the weekend. For some strange reason, he believed that I was having an affair with an imaginary man. His thoughts were absurd – and scary: He had grown paranoid.

As time passed, Jim would spend mostly every weekend at various, unknown locations, later stumbling back home on Sunday night. The only thing that I was sure of at the time was that my child was not going to be subjected to the atmosphere, be it the negativity in the flat, or around Jim when he became hostile. In time, not only would he make one unusual phone call; he began to make several, to my place of employment.

Dropping Jim off at work meant that he was stuck at the restaurant for lunch, unless one of his coworkers would take him out. In all of the months leading up to my return to work at the hospital, he had not once called me on his lunch break. As it was, I would not even find out about any changes in plans, until after I had gone to get him in the evening.

By early spring of that year, Jim began calling my direct extension at work, two and three times each day, to ask what I was doing. To this day, it's a mystery as to why he thought I was having an affair. I had no close male friends, but he would grill me as to who I was associating with while at work, and who I spoke with on a regular basis.

Jim also wanted to know the names of everyone in the Business Office, along with where they lived, who I ate lunch with, and even the precise times I was having lunch. Carol and I would both comment that he was behaving like a stalker, not a husband. His fear and suspicions were completely uncalled for, as well as unfounded.

Not only did his actions make me feel uncomfortable, the frequent calls warranted my Supervisor to restrict my personal calls. I was only allowed to call Sarah for sake of being my sitter, or, to use the phone for emergencies. Warning Jim to stop calling, he continued to do so until he finally got sick of my hanging up in his ear.

I was baffled. Searching for an answer, I recall a distressing conversation that we had whereas I asked him why he was behaving in such a manner. His words were chilling.

Cool, calm and strangely collected, he sneered, "I'm your husband and you're my wife. You are not *anything*, to *anyone* else." That was more than unsubstantiated jealously – it was an indirect warning.

Trying to avoid a major blowout, I sat quietly absorbing his comment, as he glared at me for a few moments, and then walked away. The statement was insane!

Later that spring, and having never mentioned why, my mother-in-law had also stated that she did not want to visit us at 207. She did, however, keep an open door policy for us to go to her home. With hindsight, I have often wondered if the handful of times that she did visit the flat, she had felt something and was too afraid to mention it. That was entirely possible, given what I had learned from Chris, and Karen.

One by one, people expressed their disliking of the flat. Only to very few could I confide in what was going on in the house. I remember how incredibly frustrating it was to be stuck there for the duration of our lease.

Meanwhile, the tension continued to steadily mount. More times than not, I would visit my in-laws, and it was just a matter of time before my mother-in-law had noticed the strain of Jim's behavior, on our relationship. She did not condone his excursions, and was outspoken about his roaming around town, for entire weekends at a time.

Understanding our difficulties, there was nothing that my mother-in-law wouldn't do within her means, to help us. That included her sending me to spend some 'alone time' with Jim, to see if it would help our relationship. Sometimes it did, while most times, it did not.

I found that our 'alone time' spent at 207, made the energies more intense. Jim's personality would flip, and he would spend most of the night watching porn in the living room; he thrived on it. In turn, his treatment of me in the bedroom was almost animalistic. Confused, and distressed by his actions, I remember thinking, *where did my husband go?*

With no way to predict his personality changes, the only common denominator was that the flat made him more belligerent, and unreasonable. Several months into our lease, and I remember feeling trapped in my own home.

* * * * * * *

Steadily on the decline, Jim's lack of ability to respect anyone, or anything, had become bewildering. An example of his unusual conduct is demonstrated by the following event.

Having been asleep for only a few hours, Jim got up and had gone to sit in the living room. Thinking that he was going to watch one of his 'movie rentals,' I remember noticing that it was just after 12:00AM, and withheld comment.

The room remained dark, free of any glow from the television that would have been cast on the walls from the direction of the front room. I also remember that it was very quiet. Just before dozing off a short while later, I also recall thinking that he had decided to sleep on the sofa.

Later, and close to 5:00AM that morning, I woke to the sound of a car door being closed, coming from the direction of the rear parking lot. Given the fact that it was a Sunday morning, I remembering sleepily questioning who would be out at that time. Unfortunately, it was not until I went to get Jimmy from the nursery, that I noticed that our car had been moved from the spot in which I had parked it, the night before.

That was when it dawned on me: Jim had taken the car after I had fallen back to sleep, earlier that morning. I hypothesized that the car door that I heard around 5:00AM, was Jim coming home. Never once did I notice any noise in the flat. He had managed to sneak out, and then back in to the house – undetected.

Sure enough, after going outside to inspect the car for damage, I found an empty beer can resting on the backseat. Not only was he driving with a suspended license, someone been drinking in it, too! I remember feeling hurt, and angry. I could not understand why he was acting in such an irresponsible manner.

I talked to Carol, Karen and my mother about it: Nothing made any sense, and he was beginning to exhibit self-destructive behavior. We all agreed that it was best not to confront Jim while he was under the influence, but in the meantime, it was agreed that I had to look for any possible clues as to indicate what was going on.

During the early afternoon of that same day, I took Jimmy with me to speak with Len and Sarah at their house. I knew that Len was very close to Jim, and thought perhaps he would have some insight.

Both denied hearing anything out of the ordinary. Good news there, but when I asked about drugs, Len only stated that he knew Jim had been drinking hard liquor – and in excessive quantities. This was somewhat unusual, as he was typically a 'beer guy,' but afforded little explanation.

Len also offered to talk to Jim for me, due to concerns that he was spiraling out of control. Len also confessed to knowing that Jim had been taking the car for at least *two months* prior, and felt very badly about not wanting to get involved.

While concluding our conversation, and as if he had a third sense that we were talking about him, Jim walked through Len's kitchen door with an expression on his face that looked like he had heard every single word we had said. Exchanging glances, it was easy to know what was going through our minds: Exactly how much, did he hear?

Disturbed, would be a good way to describe my husband's mentality at that moment. He simply asked what we were doing and then ordered me to go home and make dinner. Right then and there, I had an inkling that he was going to throw down the law with my discussing our problems with friends. As anticipated, he did just that.

Saying only a few words to me as we walked back to the house, I could sense his anger as we climbed the stairs to the flat. Situating Jimmy in his playpen, it took a matter of seconds before Jim was in the kitchen lecturing me about keeping my mouth shut. The friction in the air was so thick, that it was almost unbearable.

Trying to focus on the cooking pan in front of me, I remember turning and asking him what his problem was. That was when he told me that the only time that I was "allowed" to go to Len and Sarah's, was to drop off Jimmy in the morning, and again when it came time to pick him up after work. He also told me that he did not want my mother, Carol or Karen visiting. It was very clear that he was trying to isolate me.

His verbal attack was unexpectedly punctuated by a heart-stopping *CRASH!* I knew exactly what had happened: My ornamental art had tumbled from the wall – *again.*

Moving just a yard, or two away from me, Jim surveyed the damage; it was destroyed. My mother's beautiful gift had met its demise, and was laying in several pieces on the floor.

The disturbance provided Jim with some time to cool down, as he cleaned up the splintered wood. My instincts told me that there was something more to the decoration's repeated dives to the ground, but I avoided adding the subject to an already heated discussion. Following the short-lived interruption, I continued haggling with Jim.

I begged him to tell me why I had to stay tethered to the house; he was treating me like a hostage. After expressing my feelings to him, in addition to reminding him that he could not legally take the car, he punched the refrigerator and told me that he could do whatever he wanted to; I could not stop him. He also made it clear to me, that he didn't care what I said, or thought.

Frustrated, I finished cooking the meal and sat at the table with he and Jimmy, not speaking a word. I remember thinking that Jim was going stark, raving mad. Hard liquor or not, he was a completely different person than the man I had married. At the hands of an unseen enemy, a hostile takeover had occurred without anyone having noticed.

7

The Escape

My personal support group provided me with strength and wisdom, on how to best handle the shaky situation. Jim continued to grow more controlling, and made every effort possible, to keep me from my friends and family. I was *permitted* to visit his parents, which was really the only reprieve that I had on my weekends off.

By then, any requests to get out to spend time with Carol, or even to go visit my mother, were met with agonizing resistance, and intimidation tactics. It was not worth upsetting Jim to push the matters any further, therefore, I had resigned to quite a bit of secluded time in the foul flat.

My husband, a man who had once been nurturing of my relationship with family and friends, had become extremely suspicious of them. Most contact with the outside world aside from work had been reduced to strategic phone conversations when Jim was not at home.

Fortunately, Carol and I began to carpool, so that provided a welcome opportunity for us to chat outside of a shared lunch. Once in a blue moon, and only after picking up Jimmy, would we bravely scoot off to the mall, or out to have dinner. Taking Jim's schedule into consideration, I was able to spend a little bit more time with Sarah after work.

Aware of the restrictions that Jim had imposed, she too, began to express concern. Sarah's apprehension would reach an entirely new level, after bearing witness to the following:

As was characteristic of our carpooling during the week, Carol had dropped me off at Sarah's. On this particular day, I do not remember having spent more than twenty minutes visiting with her, before returning home with Jimmy. From the outside, nothing appeared to be out of the ordinary, but I recall my surprise as I walked through the door of the flat, and found Jim sitting in the living room! No television or radio had been turned on; he was planted on the couch with a stone-cold look on his face.

Knowing how he felt about me visiting with friends, this was a situation that presented the need exercise extreme caution. Not wanting to make matters worse, I continued to go about my business with the baby, as he turned and watched me in silence. I also recall sensing the presence of the male spirit in the living room; I knew he was there.

I next recall heading into the nursery, to ready Jimmy for dinner. After preparing his meal, I had positioned myself in the dining room, so I could see my husband as I fed our son his dinner. When he was finished, I put Jimmy in his playpen and cooked our supper. Jim had not spoken one word to me, since I had come through the door.

I do not think that I took more than a half dozen steps out of the nursery when Jim came stomping around the corner, stopping me dead in my tracks. Face to face, he started poking me in the shoulder, forcing me backwards, into the nursery. With every shove, he furiously screamed at me for daring to visit with Sarah. Sadly, the more that Jim yelled, the more our son cried.

Demanding that Jim settle down, and suggesting we go into the living room as not to scare Jimmy, he did back off with his verbal tirade, but took me by the arm and forcefully led me into the front room. I knew that our conversation was far from over.

Ordering me to sit down, Jim all but threw me into the couch, as he remained standing. He then told me that I was *never, ever* to go against his wishes.

Angered by his inability to see that nothing harmful was being done by visiting with Sarah, I told him that he needed to calm down, and get some help; his paranoia and temper were getting the best of him. Looking back, I know that it was not the right thing to say given the timing, but I had – and there was no taking it back. Needless to say; he went nuts.

I remember him slapping the top of my head, and crouching down towards my face as he screamed. He then unleashed his fury at the sofa cushions and pillows, throwing them all over the room. He also tipped over the coffee table, which landed with a loud *CRASH!*

In the background, our son was crying uncontrollably due to the ruckus, yet Jim would not let me leave the room to console him. Every time that I would try to get up, he blocked me. With spit droplets stinging my face as he lashed out, Jim continued on his diatribe, intermittently pushing on my chest, and smacking my arms and head: That was when I knew that I had to call the police. Reaching for the phone on the nearby end table, I noticed that it was *gone!*

I could not believe it! It took me two seconds to figure out what happened to the phone when I saw him smirk at me, as my grasp for help, came up empty handed. *He had taken the damn phone!*

Stopping his physical assault briefly enough to mock me, he told me that he was not going to give me an opportunity to call the police. Outmaneuvering him by a hair, I ran into our bedroom to use another phone, but it too, was missing.

Running towards me, he grabbed my shirt and swung me around, pulling me into the dining room, as I pleaded for him to stop. I also remember looking on the wall to make sure his grandfather's .12 gauge shotgun was still locked in the gun rack. Thankfully, it was, but I still needed to get to Jimmy and leave

207, before things continued to escalate.

Urging him to stop so I could help Jimmy, only made Jim more violent. I could clearly see that he was enjoying the torture he had been inflicting on me. With a brazen smile, he informed me that he was "going to teach me a lesson."

Jimmy continued to cry in the nursery, as I kept begging for him to let me go and get our son. Figuring that I had no way of calling anyone, he pushed me through the kitchen and into the nursery, stopping just short of the door. I recall the sickening feeling as he propelled me through the kitchen: I noticed that he had also removed the kitchen phone!

It was dark and cold, and had been raining all day long. I remember picking up Jimmy from his crib and looking out into the parking lot below, and then next door to Len and Sarah's. I knew that I had to get out and call the police before something very bad happened. During the time that I was trying to comfort Jimmy, I had noticed that my husband had stormed off towards the front of the house.

With Jimmy in my arms, I stepped out into the hallway. A couple of feet farther into the kitchen and I was able to look around the corner, into the front of the flat. Sitting with his back to me, leaning forward with his head bowed down and his hands wrapped around the sides of his head, I knew that I had to escape.

Inching forward, as quietly as could be, I snuck past the kitchen entryway towards the backdoor, opened it, and without even shutting the door behind me, ran down the stairs as fast as I could. Indeed, it was a bold attempt, but it was a risk that I was willing to take.

In the midst of the cold, pouring rain, with nothing on my feet, and my son wearing only a pair of fleece pajamas, I dashed through the dark, cutting through our small backyard. I also vividly remember making the split-second decision to take the longer route towards the front of Len and Sarah's, instead of the rear entrance. I knew that Jim would have a bird's eye view of me going inside, had he gone to the kitchen window to look for me.

Trying not to make too much noise, I fervently began to ring the doorbell. After a few rings, Len opened the door to find both Jimmy and I, soaked to the skin. It didn't take him long to figure out that something had happened.

I remember Sarah walking out of the kitchen with a quizzical look on her face. I told them Jim had removed all of the phones and had turned violent, threatening me.

Immediately, Len called the police. Due to the close proximity of the police station, it was only moments until an Officer arrived at Len and Sarah's, while other squad cars pulled up to 207.

After their initial interviews, they requested that I go over to the flat. They wanted to talk to both Jim and I, together. Len and Sarah cared for Jimmy, to keep him out of harm's way.

Entering through the front door, I was escorted up the stairs by two Officers. All of the lights had been turned on. Sitting on the couch was Jim, flanked by two more Officers. I will never forget how surreal the entire situation was, as my husband sat on the couch with that strange smile – as though once again, the whole ordeal had been a joke.

After explaining what had taken place, the police questioned Jim as why he had gone through such great lengths to come home early without my knowledge, and hide all of the telephones if he had no prior intention of harming me. His response of, "I don't know," was accented with a very weird laugh. It was not only evident to me, but to the police, as well, that my husband was not in a sound state of mind.

Running a background check, the police found that Jim had a suspended license, but that was it. Aside from a few red marks on my arms and chest, I had no other injuries.

The police also asked him if he had been drinking, or taking any drugs: Jim replied that he had not. An Officer in the dining room also inquired about the lock on the gun rack and advised Jim that he was going to check the shotgun for loaded ammunition, of which there was none.

After several more questions, they issued Jim a warning and told him that they would arrest him if he laid a hand on either

Jimmy or I, or if they were to get called back to 207. They also suggested that he leave the house and go stay with a friend, or family member for the night. Heeding their advice, he got up from the couch and pulled one of the hidden telephones out of a decorative basket that was positioned in front of the fireplace.

Making a phone call to one of his friends, he advised the police that he was leaving, and was escorted out. A short while later, Sarah brought Jimmy back to the flat.

Jim stayed with his friend for close to a week. I prayed our time apart would knock some sense into him.

During the week in which Jim was gone, I had the displeasure of staying in the house. I remember that I was worried Jim was going to snap again, and show up in one of his moods.

Fortunately, he did not, but the entire time I was home, be it before, or after work, I could not help but notice that the air in that flat was shifting again, becoming almost excessively oppressive. The presence of the male spirit energy also seemed stronger.

I remember going to sleep with my rosary beads in hand, praying to God to protect us from whatever evil was dwelling in 207. The energies were creating a volatile atmosphere fueled by dangerous emotion – and it felt as though someone was about to strike a match in the middle of a gas chamber.

* * * * * * *

One of my resources to inquire about Jim's behavior was his best friend, Jerry. I took advantage of that one afternoon after he came over to watch a ball game with Jim, at the flat. Jerry had taken Jim in on the night the police had asked him to leave 207, so any observations relative to Jim's disposition while he was not in the house, would come in handy.

Diplomatic as ever, Jerry tried to play marriage counselor, which actually helped to shed some light on what was going on in Jim's mind. As Jerry mediated, Jim apologized for undisclosed "personal issues" that he did not feel comfortable explaining. He also admitted that he was somewhat depressed, although he could not explain why. That was when Jerry asked if he was "as depressed" as he was, when a prior girlfriend had broken off their engagement. Jim answered Jerry, with what I believed to be an honest, "No."

Jerry continued to try and extrapolate information, but it was easy to see that it only frustrated Jim; he couldn't pinpoint the cause for his feelings. Very worried to learn that he had felt dejected over the breakup of an old flame in the past, I felt the need to ask if he wanted to hurt himself. Disturbed by my question, Jim replied with another, "No."

My husband also denied the fact that he needed help. With options available to get assistance, he scoffed at our suggestion. Denial was not his friend, and it was killing me inside to know that he was struggling, yet refusing treatment. At the very least, he needed to stop drinking, but even then there was quite a bit more work that would need to be done to get to the root of his troubles; he had become unhinged.

Jim explained how much he loved Jimmy and I; that we were not the cause as to why he was depressed. He also promised to stop drinking, which was something that Jerry agreed needed to be done sooner, rather than later.

Best friends since childhood, I was hoping that if anyone could reach my husband, Jerry would be the one. Thankful that some progress had been made, the only thing that was clear in such a fog of uncertainty, was the fact that Jim had been fighting some rather hefty, personal demons.

At times, he appeared to have the look of lost child, trying to find his way – a look that haunts me to recall. As much as he stated he was fine, his eyes reflected: *Please help me. I don't know what's going on.*

* * * * * * *

Carol, who was in Nursing School at the time, along with my mother who had been an R.N. for almost twenty-six years, agreed that Jim was experiencing more of a nervous breakdown than anything, and suggested that I look into his family history to see if I could find a missing link. My efforts failed in the most colossal of ways.

My in-laws stated that aside from both of Jim's brothers being hearing impaired, the only familial issue was alcoholism. They did, however, mention that they were concerned he was doing drugs, but had no proof. The drug theory also factored in as part of the mystery, but unless someone was to come forward, or he was to confess, there was no way to prove it.

Given what I did know about people who use crack, cocaine and other street drugs, it could definitely have explained some of his behavior. Known to have experimented with street drugs in his past, I was aware that my husband would periodically smoke a joint with his friends.

Upon inquiring about the use of other street drugs, Jim denied use. Without evidence, I could not just outwardly accuse him. In turn, it was agreed that so long as he did not smoke pot in the house, or in front of Jimmy, I would not interfere; what he did on his own, was his business, so long as it didn't affect my family. I also remember warning him that he was taking a big chance, by exposing himself to such dangers.

Much to my disappointment, Jim continued drinking and found a million excuses why I should be accepting of him doing so. Trying to approach the situation from a medical perspective, I recall telling him several times, that he was only damaging his liver, and shortening his lifespan. I also remember telling him that if he didn't watch it, he could even leave Jimmy fatherless. Not even those words made a difference.

I did notice that he was more receptive to spending time as a family, when we weren't at home. A random visit to Grafton State Park always boosted his spirits, and he thoroughly enjoyed the outdoor time that we would spend together. On those days, flashes of my 'old husband' would shine through. Most other times I sat at home, segregated from family and friends, questioning why he was behaving in such a way.

Come mid-March of that year, having spent so much time at home alone, I decided to inform Jim that I was thinking of taking Carol out for a small birthday dinner. Although he was not happy with this news, he did not fight it, and even offered to spend some quality time with our son. That was perfect for everyone, and showed me that perhaps he was reconsidering his treatment of me, and trying to make a change.

Jim had also promised that he would not drink while he was alone with our son, suggesting that I call and check on them both, while I was out. All for taking steps in the right direction, I agreed to the caveat of an early dinner, and made plans to celebrate with Carol, immediately after work.

I remember that it felt very good to be able to spend time with my friend. The mood was light and I refrained from talking about personal issues in an effort not to dampen her special day. Wrapping it up early as to keep the peace with Jim, we headed back to Watervliet.

It had grown dark by the time Carol had pulled up to the curb in front of 207. Upon approach, I noticed that the living room light was on, and assumed that Jim was still awake. This surprised me, as I had called to check on Jimmy while we were out. Informing me that he and our son had a nice evening, he stated that he was pretty tired and was heading to bed early. Maybe he had changed his mind?

Chatting for a few minutes from the passenger side of the car, I was looking to my left, or facing south: Carol was obviously looking in my direction, facing north. Wishing one another a goodnight, Carol happened to look up towards the house and said that it looked like Jim had become impatient. Pointing up to the window, she gave him a quick wave, as I turned to my right, and looked up. Sure enough, his tall silhouette could be seen standing in the left living room window, the lace curtains pulled to each side.

"Oh, boy!" I remember saying aloud. "Leave it to Jim; my time allotment is up. Gotta go! See you in the morning!"

As I walked up the steps, I noticed that Jim was no longer standing in front of the window. Once inside of the house, I remember making note of how quiet it was.

The hallway seemed gloomy. Sterile and aged, it had grown

to remind me of a funeral home. The dim lighting, contrasting against the dark, teal walls, contributed to more of a macabre ambiance. Having lived in the flat for several months at that time, it still seemed like each step up the stairs, was like moving closer to the Twilight Zone.

I distinctly remember putting my key in the lock and trying to turn it, but the lock would not budge. *Chink-chink, chink-chink*; I could barely turn it a hair. Never having happened in the past, I was relieved to know that Jim was on the other side of the door, and could let me in.

Knocking quietly, I waited for my husband to come to my rescue. A minute or so passed, and still no answer. I had made another attempt to turn the key; *chink-chink, chink-chink.*

Thinking that he may be sitting on the couch, which backed up to the second story landing, I tried tapping directly on the wall: Nothing. I could not imagine what he was doing, or why he could not hear me.

I was confident that he was in there; Carol and I both saw him loitering in the window. The more time that went by as I stood anxiously waiting on the landing, I remember wondering if he was playing a prank, or was busy in the bathroom.

After trying to get his attention for several minutes, I thought; to heck with trying to be quiet, I need to get in my house! *Rap, rap, rap…rap, rap, rap!*

"Jim! Please open the door! My key won't work! Please let me in! This isn't funny!" I called out.

I would say that a total of no more than 10 minutes had passed since the time Carol and I saw him in the window, to the last time I knocked on the door and called his name. Exasperated, I decided to wait a few more minutes before giving it another try, just in case he had been indisposed in the bathroom.

Taking a seat on one of the stairs, I remember my first floor neighbor opening his door and asking if everything was O.K. I told him that my key was not working, but I knew Jim was in the flat, and probably in the bathroom. He then politely offered for me to use his phone, should I remain unsuccessful with my knocking endeavor.

Standing back up, I gave another heavy pounding. *Thump, thump, thump...thump, thump, thump...*"Jim! Are you in there?" I cried.

Just as I turned to head down to Vinny's, the door flew wide open. Vinny then shut his door, as I walked into the flat, questioning what had taken my husband so long.

With his dark, brown hair piled in a disheveled mess on top of his head, and with sleep lines indenting his cheek, it was obvious that he had just woken up. He then stated that he had been asleep for close to two hours.

I then asked how that was possible, as several minutes beforehand he had been standing in the living room window. I could tell by the look on his face, that he had no idea what I was talking about.

Explaining to Jim that Carol had noticed him first, and had waved, I went on to tell him that I too, had clearly viewed him in the window. Annoyed that I had been banging on the door and had woken our neighbor, he grumbled that we were "seeing things," and went back to sleep. I headed over to the nursery to check on Jimmy.

I remember that Jimmy was sound asleep in his crib, undisturbed by my knocking. With an unsettling feeling rising in my gut, I wanted to know who was standing in the window. Had Jim been sleepwalking? I had to give Carol a call and let her know what had taken place.

Waiting enough time for her to get back home, I did just that: I recall that she was just as dumbfounded as I was. The only rational explanation that we could think of was that Jim had wandered to the window in his sleep. And that's when it hit me...

"Oh, my God!" I blurted out. "Chris! He had those crazy dreams about the man trying to force him out the door and window!"

It just so happened to be the very same window that we had found Chris at, the last time he had slept on the couch. I had goose bumps all over my body. Was that man coming to Jim in his dreams, trying to get him to do the same? Was this the same man whose energy I could sense, prowling about the flat?

I was shocked. I was convinced more than ever, that our house was experiencing more than a little bit of paranormal activity: It was like a full-fledged, haunted freak show!

The next morning I was eager to find out if Jim could recall having any strange dreams. Insisting that he had not, he stated once more, that Carol and I must have been seeing things. Carol would later tell Jim that she and I both, saw the *same thing*. We were certain, without one single doubt, that someone – a man – had been standing in that window before I got out of the car, and that it looked like Jim.

* * * * * * *

I tried to get to the local library to see if I could pull up any archived information on the house, but never had the opportunity to get there, and do the research. I wasn't keen on calling the Landlord, as I really didn't think that he would tell me anything. Even if something did happen in the house, he would probably not disclose the information for fear he could lose good Tenants.

In the meantime, my grandmother had just returned from a lengthy overseas trip to Poland, and Italy. With a coveted photograph capturing her spontaneous meeting with the Pope while standing in the crowd, she insisted that she and my mother come pay us a visit. This would present a tricky situation, as Jim did not want anyone coming over to the flat. I was lucky enough to have gone out for dinner with Carol on her birthday, and was going to be pushing it.

I was met with opposition as I told Jim that my grandmother was in town, and had wanted to stop by. He moaned and complained that he did not want anyone in the house, but explaining that it had been a long time since she saw little Jimmy, he was more apt to mull it over.

Agreeing to *his terms* not to talk about our personal business, I was thrilled when he conceded to let them come over.

Considering he had approved their visit without a big to-do, he walked away rather agitated.

The following day was lovely! What surprised me more than anything was the fact that my grandmother was willing to come over, choosing to ignore her feelings about 207. She would later disclose that the house did bother her, but she did not want it to prevent her from visiting her great grandson, and I. She adored all of her great-grandchildren, but Jimmy was quite special; he had been born on her birthday.

I recall Jim answering the door, and being somewhat aloof in disposition. He let them into the flat, and showed them to the living room while I went to get Jimmy from the nursery. Turning away from the two after greeting them both with a big hug and kiss, I noticed an unusual look on my grandmother's face as she stood in the middle of the room: I remember wondering if she had noticed the haze. I also could not help but feel she had honed-in on the energies. Regardless, there was little doubt she was on to something.

Upon returning to the front room with Jimmy, my grandmother was unloading her bags and chattering about what a wonderful trip she had taken. My husband, uninterested, sat in the chair, chomping at the bit. We all could see that he was more than annoyed.

One of the trip's highlights was going to the Vatican, to see Pope John Paul II. She was in her glory to have had a picture taken, as she reached out to touch the Pope's hand. Rustling through her bag of trinkets, the photo was one of the first things she pulled out.

I remember that when it came time for Jim to take a look at the photo, he brushed it away. I recall my grandmother being quite offended by his gesture, and insisted that he look at it. She then placed it on his knees.

Becoming more angered with her persistence, Jim pushed it off his lap and stormed out of the room, stating that he was sick of listening to our "crap." I remember feeling so hurt for my grandmother, as she was only trying to show him something that meant a great deal to her.

For some unknown explanation, he wanted nothing to do with it – or us for that matter – and had no trouble making that known. The look on my grandmother's face was one of hurt, as well as question, as if she was trying to figure out why he was so unreceptive about the photograph.

Picking it up from the floor, she showed me the photo and expressed what a poignant, life memory that moment had become. As she spoke, I recall her tone had changed from one of excitement, to that of being wounded undoubtedly, by Jim's little outburst.

As my husband's behavior continued to deteriorate, the atmosphere in the house became quite uncomfortable. We could hear him talking to himself, making snide remarks as he wandered around. He had also gone into the bedroom and had shoved one of the draws closed, causing the three of us to jump.

My grandmother, known to be very direct in approach, asked Jim to return to the living room, but he declined. That was when she got up and met him in the dining room. It was clear that she felt slighted, and given the fact she had traveled quite a distance to visit, she was upset with him.

Giving him a piece of her mind for being treated so rudely, she asked my husband what his issue was. Replying that he felt no need to explain, only added fuel to the fire. That was when Jim had enough of the confrontation, and abruptly left the house on foot.

Embarrassed and disappointed by his attitude, I apologized for his actions, as my grandmother sat and quietly played with Jimmy. I remember that she told me that I should not apologize for him – that it was not my fault.

Curious as to why he had slammed the drawer, I went into the bedroom and found that he had accessed one of *my* drawers, which had bounced back open. Catching my eye was the tip of a brown object resting on some of my clothes. Sliding it out, I had realized my husband had taken our cross off the wall over our bed, and had thrown it my dresser! For the life of me, I could not understand why he had done such a spiteful thing! I assumed it had to do with my grandmother raving about meeting the Pope, but even then, it seemed like an awfully crude thing to do.

Not wanting him to break it, I thought it was best to leave it in my drawer. He was pissed off about something, and I remember his unwarranted actions had made me sad to know that he was so angry, and unhappy.

A short while after returning to the front room, my grandmother stood up, handed Jimmy to my mother and said, "Michaeline, Jill Marie…I want to get out of here. Let's go out for dinner."

As we made our way to the restaurant, she then explained that the house was "no good," and stated that she did not like it *at all*. In her words, she described it as something not being "right in there," and did not want to go back. In tears, due in part of her scaring me and validating my own feelings, I was also disappointed that both Jim and the house had managed to create another rift. From Chris, to Karen, and now my dear grandmother – all three of them did not want to stay at our home.

Refusing to elaborate, she wanted to focus on enjoying the rest of the day. My mother and I could tell she was greatly disturbed.

Later that evening, I poured over everything that had happened since our move to the flat, trying to understand what may be going on. It always came down to my wondering if someone had died in the house, as I contemplated if their spirit was not at rest.

The only alternative that I had left, was to enlist the help of Father. It was going to be a major decision that would require a great deal of courage, as I would have to take full responsibility if Jim were to find out.

Taking a day, or so, to muster my strength for the daring move, I called and left a message with the secretary, asking that Father give me a call. I also told her to make a note that Father should not mention my message to Jim. She agreed to relay the information, and stated that he would more than likely return the call within a day or so, as he was busy. I specifically avoided giving her any pertinent details.

Two days passed, without word from Father. Another week passed – and still no call. I decided to make one more attempt to reach him and was again, greeted by the secretary. Stating that it was pretty important for Father to get a hold of me, I asked if he could expedite a return call.

I knew that Father was an extremely busy man. He was well-liked and always very involved with the community, therefore, it did not come as a surprise that he did not return the first call. However, come another week after leaving the second message without hearing back, my hopes were dashed. I felt helpless, and grasped at straws trying to figure out why he had not responded.

Low and behold, the saga of Father's messages came to a rip-roaring conclusion one evening, after picking up Jim at work. Boy, was he was livid!

To this very day, I still have no clue as to how he found out. Approximately two days after I had left my last message with the rectory secretary, Jim found out that I had called, and asked to speak with Father.

The only thing that I can think of is my mother-in-law, who was always in church, (and very close to Father), may have been asked by his secretary, as to why I was calling. Innocent enough, I am only able to surmise that in turn, my concerned and unknowing mother-in-law, may have asked Jim what was going on, prompting him to put a stop to things before they went any further. Again, this is something that I cannot validate, but speculate as the cause.

Regardless, Jim's cocky attitude about preventing the contact and blessing, was extremely upsetting. With no surprise, he reminded me that I had gone behind his back, and retaliated with a full-scale verbal attack, during the drive home.

In agreement about the obvious, I stood my ground and tried to offer him an explanation for my actions. He didn't care and ridiculed my concern, stating that there was nothing wrong with the house or flat – he didn't want to hear about it. He also warned me to *never* to go behind his back like that again.

Exhausting all avenues to reach out for help, I remember the harsh realization that I was in it alone. No longer could I count on my husband to be part of the solution: I had to rely on myself, and do the best that I could, given the escalating situation at hand.

8

A Shell Remains

The spring weather had shaped up nicely. I recall being more than happy to be able to keep the apartment windows open, in order to air-out the place. Strangely, aside from any attempts to rid the flat of that unpleasant feeling, the damn haze would hang in the living room, undisturbed by even the breeziest of days.

With Jim's drinking on the rise, so were his escapades and weekend getaways. Bowling nights were typically the most difficult, and almost routine: His friend would pick him up and he would come home either incredibly happy, or in a major funk – intoxicated each time.

On bowling nights, I remember making sure to be fast asleep by the time he came back home, as a means to avoid his wrath. His drinking problem further exacerbated his Dr. Jekyll, and Mr. Hyde persona, making it very difficult to predict what kind of evening I would be in for.

I cannot recollect the exact date, but know that it was an unseasonably warm night, when Jim had stumbled into the flat after bowling. He was quite inebriated.

Intending to create a disturbance, my husband made a huge amount of noise, as he sang loudly and talked to himself in the kitchen, and then moved into the front room. I knew that it was just a matter of time until he would wake up Jimmy. It was close to 1:00AM, and I had little doubt that our downstairs neighbor Vinny, would also become a casualty of Jim's commotion.

Sure enough, I heard Jimmy cry out from his nursery and got up to tend to him. I recall standing over his crib, patting his back, trying to hush him back to sleep, as Jim quieted down.

Hoping to get some more shuteye and avoid a full-blown fiasco, I headed back to bed. In passing, I had noticed that Jim had changed his clothes, as if he was getting ready to leave the house.

Asking where he was headed off to, I remember hearing him mumble that he was "going out." Concerned about his mode of transportation, I asked him if someone was waiting outside. In a very cutting tone, he advised me that he was going to take the car!

Oh, no, he wasn't – not if I could help it! I could not let my husband just walk out the door in his condition, and take the car. Not only was he drunker than a skunk, he had a suspended license!

Trying to calmly remind him of these facts, he stated that he didn't "give a shit," and continued into the kitchen to make a snack. Thinking quick, I went into the dining room, took the keys out of my handbag, and hid them. That turned out to be a very bad, and extremely dangerous mistake.

As Jim finished munching on a sandwich, he headed straight to my bag and began to rifle through it. Unable to find the keys in my usual spot, he looked in the kitchen and then realized that I had hid them.

Standing in our bedroom doorway, I watched his expression change from that of happy drunk, to something that I still have a difficult time explaining. Everything about his whole state of being became altered. That was when he turned to me, and asked if I had the keys. My response: I was not going to give them to him.

I do not remember much other than him coming towards me with a crazed look on his face, acting like a mad man – and then being knocked down, onto the floor. Punching me in the face, he continued by slamming my head into the carpet.

What I do remember is thinking that I was going to die. He had turned into a monster: A vile, evil monster – over a set of car keys. I also remember fearing for little Jimmy, should he manage to kill me.

He continued beating me like a punching bag for three minutes or so, until I finally told him where they were. Hearing him leave the flat once he finished the assault, I was barely able to sit up, my head spinning, and my body aching.

The police arrived very shortly thereafter, and attempted to look for him. He had somehow managed to disappear into the night. Logically, the Officers advised me leave with Jimmy, for sake of our safety. They did not have to tell me twice: I was out of there.

One of the Officers took Jimmy and I to the police station, where I filled out a report and made arrangements to go to Carol and Kathy's apartment, in Brunswick. Physically, I was going to be all right, despite having a fat lip, some scrapes and bruises, while emotionally, I was drained. The sheer thought of the fiendish look in his eyes, made me quake.

Eventually, the police were able to arrest Jim after he returned to the flat. He was charged with assault and battery, evidently leaving the car behind to avoid being found. This entire ordeal signaled a new battle: Regardless of how much I loved him, I could not stay in the relationship.

Jimmy and I stayed with Carol and Kathy for close to a week, during which time I tried to come up with a plan to keep us safe. The very thought of going back to 207 made me sick, while the change in environment – being away from the flat and the energies – made me feel much better. There was now little room for question; the energies were negatively influencing my family, and seemed to be devouring my husband at warp speed.

Out of fear that I would lose my job if we were to go to trial, I agreed to drop the charges during his court appearance. I remained nervous about the whole situation, having no idea what he was going to do next. I knew that I was taking a huge gamble.

I believe that it had been close to a month that we had been living apart: He, staying with one of his friends, and I, returning to the flat. Jim was not happy with the arrangements, but he needed help, and this was the only option.

* * * * * * *

What a person may be willing to do for sake of saving their marriage is often influenced with the heart, rather than the head. I can see this relative to my marriage with Jim, accepting responsibility for my own decisions for sake of one last attempt to salvage our relationship. I had not yet given up hope and was willing to see if there was any way possible that I could reach my husband, and pull him out of his cascading slump.

Taking great care to evaluate our telephone conversations and Jim's appeal to consider an apology, I could 'hear' my husband making an effort to reach out. It would be a decision that was ultimately, made in haste.

With many late night talks, and just a few months remaining on our lease, I remember thinking that I would be able to hang on long enough to get away from 207 19th Street, and give our marriage an opportunity to heal in a new environment. I had to do what I could, without completely walking away from my husband. In my heart, I had to give him the benefit of the doubt.

Back together no more than a week, or so, proved to be an incredibly trying period of time. Sadly, I found out that Jim was drinking on the side, and trying to hide it. It was painfully evident that he was not going to get the help he needed, and I could see that he was sliding into a state of oblivion.

Admittedly, it was my own damn fault for listening to my heart, but God knew that I had the right intentions. I had to put my best foot forward, and accept the fact that had he made one move to signal he may become violent, I was going to leave *for good.*

Carol and I continued to have lunch together, keeping one another abreast as to what was happening in our lives. Having truly been grateful for the time that Jimmy and I stayed with her and Kathy, I had realized that some friends are more like family, and that was the case with Carol: She, Karen and Kathy, were to me, like sisters that I never had. In fact, her entire family was an exemplary model of unconditional love that I greatly respected, and still do, to this very day.

One of Carol's favorite things to do (and still is) was to share quality recipes. During our brief stay with her, she had put one of those recipes to use, creating a mouthwatering dish of Lemon Chicken. Out of this world, and incredibly scrumptious, I raved over the masterpiece and had to have the recipe. Deciding to jot it down at a later date, it wasn't until weeks later, and after Jim and I had reconciled, that she presented it to me, during one of our lunch breaks. I knew that Jim would enjoy it, and could hardly wait to make it for him.

Following a quick stop to fetch Jim at the restaurant, I dashed into Price Chopper, to pick up last-minute ingredients for the feast. Pleased with the meal plan, I remember Jim being in a fairly good mood, as we then headed over to Sarah's to pick up Jimmy.

A Cook himself, Jim was always pouring over recipes and making up his own, so after having gotten Jimmy settled on the floor for some playtime, I took out the instructions, and showed them to him. He perused it for a minute, or two, before placing it onto the coffee table.

Returning to the kitchen to prepare Jimmy's bottles, I remember a distinct change in Jim's disposition within moments after walking through the apartment door. As much as he would never admit it, I knew that 207 bothered him; the question was, *"Why?"*

Come time to start dinner, I had realized that the recipe was on the coffee table in the front room. Walking through the dining room, towards the front of the house, I saw Jim sitting on the floor, doing silly dad things, with our son. How I had wished Jim could just have snapped out of it – how I wished we had never moved in to Hell.

I can still remember walking up to the coffee table and noticing that the recipe was not there. Positive that Jim had moved it, I inquired to its whereabouts, only to be met with a confused look on Jim's face. I could see his genuine surprise that it was not there, even becoming quick to explain that he did not take it. The two of us stared at one another knowing fully well, that the yellow piece of legal paper with Carol's handwriting, had been sitting there thirty minutes or so, earlier.

I recall frantically checking my pockets, and Jim had even gotten up to check his. With the both of us searching for the recipe, cushions were checked, the rug was lifted and my pocketbook was inspected, yet still no recipe. It had vanished! Retracing our steps did not produce a hint as to where it had gone.

We had a mystery on our hands. In my opinion, one of two things had transpired: Either Jim was playing a rotten trick on me, or the recipe had truly disappeared. Trying to remember what the recipe had stated, I was not going to let it spoil dinner.

Mystified and annoyed, I did my best to make the Lemon Chicken. Not convinced it had just grown legs, gotten up and walked away on its own, I hated thinking that Jim had pulled a fast one. Suffice to say, it was a weird situation, and be it known; the recipe was never found.

* * * * * * *

When it rains, it pours. Just when I thought that matters could not possibly become more complicated, or get any worse, they did.

It all started when our cat Pooh, figured out a way to flee the flat. I had not seen him try to leave, and as much as Jim was willing to admit, he had not noticed either. Reminiscent of the recipe, Pooh had vanished without a trace, and for two agonizing weeks, we searched for him to no avail. I thought for sure that I would never see him again. Compounding Pooh's disappearance was another puzzling incident, once again, taking place in the dining room.

Spending an hour or so every weekend, I would iron my attire for the workweek. Setting up the ironing board alongside the east dining room wall, I collected my clothes and hangars, situating them on the bedroom doorknob, after each piece was pressed.

Beginning as I had many times in the past, I erected the board, plugged in the iron and fetched a pile of blouses, one of which was a favorite that Carol had given to me. With the iron to my right, and a cup of distilled water on the table in front of me, I remember positioning the shirt on the nose of the board, and smoothing out the material with my hands. All that I recall was reaching for the iron to press the shirt, and dodging flames, as they surprisingly shot out from the holes on the bottom of the grating!

Spitting and sputtering, small balls of fire and spark caught the shirt as I quickly tugged on the cord to unplug it from the wall, and then doused the blouse with the distilled water. I had never seen anything like it! Yanking the shirt from the board with one hand, and grabbing the smoking iron with the other, I ran and threw them both into the kitchen sink.

Returning to the dining room, I noticed that the ironing board cover had some small burn holes on it, and was singed over a good portion. I then added it to the pile in the sink, and gave them all a soaking to extinguish any embers smoldering in the fabric, or the on inside of the iron. It was bizarre. Shocked by the random malfunction, I made sure to tell Jim about the ordeal: I was worried we had a malfunctioning socket.

Taking care to inspect the wiring, there were no signs that the arcing iron had been caused by faulty wall wiring. Jim had even tested the socket, stating that the iron was defective and would obviously need to be replaced. I was very thankful that I had the water in front of me that day.

The entire event sticks out so vividly in my mind; it's not

everyday that you see irons do such things. Adding insult to injury, the lovely shirt that Carol had given me, was ruined.

The weather continued to remain rather pleasant and in turn, nights were more conducive for holding outdoor parties. This meant that Jim was ditching home in order to attend most functions in which he had received an invite. My duty as a mother was to make sure that Jimmy was safe, therefore declining to attend. And so, on one rather mild spring evening after he had finished his dinner, my husband proclaimed that he was going back out. Calling it an early night, I crawled into bed. It was no later than 8:00PM; Jimmy's customary bedtime.

Whether he managed to take the car keys before he left the house, or whether he came back to the flat while I was in a dead sleep, I will never know. Either way, he had somehow managed to get his hands on the car keys, and had taken off with the car.

I remember waking up close to 10:00PM that night, when I woke with the feeling that I should perform a visual check of the car, from the nursery. Exhausted, and nearly dismissing the thought, I climbed out of bed and went to the window: That was when I noticed the car was gone!

A thousand scenarios began to unfold in my mind. I did not know what to do, other than to wait, as I had absolutely no idea where he went.

They say that a watched kettle never boils, and for the most part, I would agree. Pacing back and forth for what seemed like hours, I would periodically check the windows for any signs of his arrival. I also remember telling myself that I needed to avoid saying, or doing anything that would make him frenzied, once he did return.

Lighting a white candle in the living room had become second nature for me whenever I was going to spend any amount of time in that awful room. My grandmother had always told me that it was good for spiritual protection and given the very unique events that had transpired in 207, I was going to do whatever I could to keep the seedy energies at bay. Nervous and disappointed that he had absconded with the car

yet again, I sat watching the candlelight, praying for my
husband – along with anyone else that would cross his path
while on the road.

I recall thinking about the energies in the flat during the
quiet of the night. I sensed the man in black might have been
both physically, and sexually abusive, during his lifetime given
the change in my husband's behavior. For certain, the energy
was born from a sick, and sadistic individual, who was for some
reason, conducting his reign of afterlife terror, in my home.

There also seemed to be an element of disguise surrounding
at least the male energy. I felt as though he was dualistic in
nature, as though he embodied two conflicting sets of values.
This bothered me greatly, as I could see Jim struggling between
right and wrong, almost as though he was being played by the
male's energy.

The unidentified energy was indeed, more terrifying than
that of the male. I sensed that it was using the male energy to
do its dirty deeds, deriving great pleasure by unleashing its
exploitive behaviors in the flat. From aggression, brutal
hostility, to full fledged masochism, it thrived on extreme
iniquity. Together, both energies were scummy and outright
disgusting to sense, hence my reasons for blocking them and
wanting them out of 207.

It was during some of those very thoughts, when I had
noticed red and blue lights bouncing off of the walls of the
Pizza Parlor, next door. I knew that they had something to do
with Jim and it wasn't too long afterward, when my suspicions
were confirmed.

Looking out of the left living room window, I saw that he
had been pulled over, very close to the house. I recall a sense of
relief knowing that he would be taken off the streets. I also
remember praying that this would scare him straight.

Not too terribly long after they had pulled him over, I heard
our doorbell ring. One of the Officers informed me that they
were taking Jim to the police station.

Due to his prior DUI, driving with a suspended license and
a newly failed sobriety test, he was in a world of trouble. I do

not remember how long he stayed in jail, but I recall his reaction to the debacle: He was fuming.

Reminding him once more that this was of his own doing, he refused to straighten up. It was time to start distancing myself from the treachery he had been creating.

Unable to justify my staying in the marriage if he was not going to seek professional help, I finally had to open the dialogue to filing for a separation. As much as it tore me apart, it was not a healthy, or safe environment for Jimmy, and I. Feeling that his self-destructive behavior was becoming a daily way of life for him, I knew that it wouldn't be long until he crossed the point of no return.

The only good news: A neighbor who lived across the street had asked if we were missing a fluffy, beige cat. Sure enough, amidst chaos and turmoil, little Pooh had been found and safely returned, only to resume taking cover in the nursery, or on my bed.

* * * * * * *

Jim did not want a separation. My mother tried to talk sense into him and get him to see the very grave situation at hand, to no avail. Any attempt to steer him towards seeking help, met with a struggle.

Jim also started to miss work, which was extremely out of character for him. A hard worker, aside from leaving early once in a great while, he would stay sober for his employ, barely missing a beat. I can't even remember him calling in sick – not even once. Thus, my grounds for worry when I found he had come home early on not one, but two occasions. One of those times he had picked up Jimmy from Sarah's; however, the last time he did not.

Climbing the stairs with Jimmy in arm, I remember opening the door and immediately sensing that Jim was home. I could feel something very different in the air, which was usually the case when Jim was home alone. Catching a quick glimpse of him as I turned and walked into the kitchen with Jimmy, I recall he was fidgeting with something on the sofa. I continued on my way, and placed Jimmy in the playpen.

Feeling the need to talk to him and find out what was going on, I warily approached Jim. I stood poised in front of him, in case I had to make a dash to safety.

"I can't do this any more," he spluttered, with tears in his eyes.

I wanted him to open up to me: I remember letting him know that he could tell me anything without fear of being judged – *anything at all.* I also told him that I wanted him to get better; he needed to come clean about what was tormenting his poor soul.

At first, he sat motionless on the couch, as more tears welled in his eyes. He was not saying a word. Worried that things could take an ugly turn, I looked around for the phone and noticed that *it was missing.* I remember becoming nauseated upon the discovery, my heart beating like a racehorse; at least I wasn't sitting down. Although he was not angry, I could see that he was extremely depressed.

I looked over towards the gun rack in the dining room, and noticed the rifle locked in place. That made me feel somewhat better, but knowing that the phone was gone, warranted an uneasy feeling. I considered sitting down next to him but knew that I would be at a considerable disadvantage, if I had to go get Jimmy.

Jim then began to ramble about many things that had been weighing heavily in his heart, and on his mind. I remember how shocked I was to hear him freely detail some brutal childhood events. Once he began to get them off of his chest, the emotional floodgates opened, as he continued to divulge some *extremely* personal information.

His bottled-up pain was mind-blowing, as he confessed to years of physical, emotional and mental abuse. I felt so, so sorry for him, and recall fighting back my own tears as he continued to vent.

Included in that conversation, he had also mentioned that he felt as though something was *wrong* with him, by which he stated that he could not explain. I thought that he was trying to describe the disease of depression, but it became apparent that there was more to it.

Intermittently, he would stop in the midst of a sentence, and tell me how much he loved Jimmy and I. It was absolutely heartbreaking to see him in such a vulnerable state.

Crying and confused, he described a fear of losing Jimmy and I. He also expressed remorse for his actions of the last several months, confessing that he felt as though he was on a one-way course to destruction.

Through his admissions, it was clear that he had been battling some serious issues, for a very long time. I also knew that moving into that apartment made things much worse than they had ever been for him, and was angry myself, that we had moved to 207. I was – and still am certain – that had we not relocated to that flat, we would not have gone through so much drama – so much pain.

It was excruciating to listen to him declare his horrific past. He had been holding back all of those emotions and experiences for so many, many years that I was in awe of how he even managed to pull it off for as long as he had. My dear twenty-five-year-old husband had endured more gut wrenching, sickening hardship, than anyone I had ever known.

During his recount, Jimmy had started to fuss; Jim had been talking for quite a while. I recall asking my husband to wait a moment, while I fixed our son something to eat, telling him that I would be right back. Pausing long enough to acknowledge my intent, he wiped his face with his t-shirt, and sat quietly on the couch as I headed towards the nursery. I remember hearing him blow his nose several times, as I prepared Jimmy's meal.

Just about ready to sit my son in his high chair, I noticed the shotgun was missing from the gun rack; the key left dangling in the lock. I remember coming to a halt, holding Jimmy as I looked towards the living room and saw Jim, with the barrel of the shotgun, pointing at his face: I had to get out.

Turning around, I literally ran out the back door one more

time, while holding onto Jimmy for dear life. I remember being completely terrified that he was going to shoot himself.

Arriving on the front porch in hysterics, I told Sarah what was going on. I cannot remember who called the police, but I do remember Sarah had taken Jimmy upstairs into one of the bedrooms, away from the chaos.

Not wanting to give him notice, the police did not sound their sirens, as several squad cars rolled up from different angles, and surrounded 207. I was instructed to stay at Sarah's.

Seconds seemed like minutes, and minutes seemed like hours. I *prayed, and prayed, and prayed* that I would not hear a gunshot. I prayed that they would get to my husband before he had the chance to do anything.

Minutes later, an Officer in 207, radioed the Officer who was stationed at Sarah's, stating that they had secured Jim's gun, and requested that I go over to the flat. Scared out of my mind, Sarah stayed with Jimmy. I had no idea what to expect. All that I knew was that he was O.K. – and that was good enough.

Entering the living room, Jim was still sitting on the sofa. I also recall one of the Officers had been inspecting the shotgun. Jim, still teary-eyed, was coherent, but solemn in character.

I recall the empathy that I felt in knowing that he bravely had worn his heart on his sleeve, but was also aware of the fact that it was an apparent last-minute confession before he contemplated ending his life. I also remember that I had to withhold comment, as I wanted to just shake him and make him snap out of it! It was killing me to see him that way!

Asked about our conversation, I provided the Officers with the details. Jim did not disagree, but I do remember him making a statement that contradicted the look in his eyes. He told the police that he wasn't really going to hurt himself, or anyone else for that matter, but was merely looking at the gun, thinking about his deceased grandfather.

Bologna! I knew that was not true. I was astonished that he managed to fool the police, and not just one: Several.

There he was, a grown man, with bloodshot, swollen eyes, saying that he was not despondent. It baffled me then, and baffles me now. Adding in the fact they found him with the gun in his hands, and after admitting to being depressed, how could they not see that he was at risk?

That was the defining second in my opinion, that Jim had crossed a very thin line. I could no longer justify living in the house with him, and stated my feelings to the police. In agreement, they suggested that it was best for Jimmy and I to leave.

Appreciative for a mini-counseling session, I remember being very concerned that they were going to allow him another opportunity to try and hurt himself. Regardless of what they believed; he was suicidal.

After receiving a stern warning and another lengthy lecture, the Officers explained that they would not arrest him, or take him in for evaluation. They did, however, take his grandfather's gun for safekeeping, due in part to his recent arrests.

Somehow, considering he had been arrested for assault and battery earlier in the year, they had failed to make him surrender his firearms. Of small consolation was the blessing that his gun was removed from the house, but I could not help but question if he would go looking for another weapon. An avid outdoorsman and hunter, he and his friends had access to many.

More than the warning he received, the fact that they were taking his grandfather's antique shotgun disturbed him most. I remember him trying to dissuade the Officers. I could sense his frustration; not only were they taking a prized family possession away from him, they were taking away his control. I also sensed that there was more trouble ahead, and the house that I had grown to despise, was going to be part of it.

I remember trying to reach out to many people, but it was of little help. Without getting in to too many details about what my husband confessed to me that day, I let my mother-in-law know what he had contemplated doing, and that police had taken his gun. I also knew that we would need to have a major talk in the future, given the details that Jim provided; however, the timing was not conducive for that.

Fearing that her son was going to do something to harm him self, or even me, my mother-in-law tried to talk to Jim, but frustration got the best of her when he told her to stay out of "his" business. I recall feeling very badly for my mother-in-law at that point: Her son was not responsive to anyone. All that she could do was make an effort to help, as so many of us had attempted to do – but failed.

That was the one, and only time, that she ever told me she did not have a "good feeling" about what was going on. Sorrowfully, I agreed. We both wanted our old Jim 'back' but the future did not look very promising: He was lost, and only a shell remained of his former sane, and loving self.

9

On The Run

With impending court dates for his arrest, I made the hard decision to compound those cases, with a legal separation, and sought counsel to begin the process. It was one of the hardest things that I have ever had to do.

In one respect, I knew that I was doing the right thing for Jimmy and I, but on the other, I knew that it was not going to help Jim's frame of mind. The only thing that I kept telling myself was that I had accepted enough apologies, and countless, empty promises. I could no longer risk my life, or Jimmy's, by trying to fix something of that magnitude.

I had asked for physical custody of our son, given the fact that I was worried about Jim's unstable behavior and drinking problem. Consulting with my lawyer, I agreed to supervised visitation until he could get some much-needed help.

Initially, Jim moved in with his best friend, Jerry, while I stayed at the flat. Getting closer to the end of our lease, I had every intention of moving out of that decrepit house, and starting over.

Come our first session in court, Jim had grown quite angry

over the ruling relative to the Temporary Order, but had done nothing to help paint him self in a positive light. A number of serious offenses, and a confession to alcohol abuse only reaffirmed the Judge's decision to maintain supervision; safety was a necessity.

Immediately following the Temporary Order, Jim began to make threatening phone calls. Not feeding into them, I would hang up on every one of his calls when he would start in. Unnerving, I had to remain focused for the sake of our son. That entailed keeping things as normal as possible for Jimmy.

I remember one evening in particular, just after our separation, when I was in the nursery, rocking Jimmy to sleep. I had been rattled by Jim's relentless calls.

Normally, the energies of 207 were primarily concentrated in the front part of the house, very rarely oozing into the back. On that night, while I was in the rocker holding Jimmy, I sensed the rotten spirit of the man, standing in the doorway. Evident to me, it seemed to have gained enough strength to pour out into the addition. This angered me; I did not want it in my son's room.

That was the evening that I look back, and vividly remember preparing myself for a *spiritual war*. I was not going to let whatever evil forces sucked the life out of our flat and my husband, take my son. I was also not going to show any fear. I knew that my belief in God, goodness and love, was much stronger than 'it' would ever be: It was time to make a stand.

With Jimmy in my arms, I went into my bedroom, took out the holy water, and began blessing the flat one more time, demanding that all evil, leave. Methodically, I moved from room to room, in an attempt to drive out the energies.

Exhausted from the ritual, I remember falling asleep in the nursery, keeping a watchful eye over my son. 'It' may have been able to attack my husband, but it wasn't going to do any more harm.

Nightly, I would pray to God for guidance and protection, and also asked Him to help my husband. With the energy remaining very oppressive, even having conducted the second blessing, it seemed to be posturing for a standoff.

Since we had not developed any type of child support protocol at the time, I was relying on my income, only. To make matters worse, Jim was fired from his job at the Tavern. The closer it came to the lease renewal, the more it looked like I was going to move in with my mother. Jim had been staying at Jerry's, as well as his parents, still upset about our separation.

One afternoon, he called and asked if he could come over to talk – I refused. I felt that it was best he kept his distance until he could show me that he was taking care of himself and making a true effort to turn his life around. I also remember being completely caught off-guard when he showed up at 207, later that afternoon.

Yelling obscenities, he tried throwing his weight against the back door. I picked up the phone and called the police, fearing for my life. Hearing my escalating voice on the phone, he backed-off and ran down the stairs; the police arriving in what seemed like mere seconds.

With signs showing that he had attempted to break into the apartment, the police began to look for him. Gathering details, some of the Officers secured the house while others scattered about downtown Watervliet.

Approximately 20 minutes later, one of the Officers reported that an Officer had cornered Jim inside the Stewart's Shop located on 19th Street. They also stated that upon approach, Jim lunged at the Officer and had attempted to punch him, before fleeing the store.

What a nightmare. If my husband was despondent enough to try and assault a cop, it was only a matter of time before he was going to kill me.

Maybe an hour later, Jim had managed to make his way back to 207. With one Officer positioned in the flat, another Officer had been outside, patrolling the perimeter. All that I recall was hearing someone yell, "HEY! HEY! HEY! GET DOWN!" from the back of the house.

Jim had evaded the police and taken refuge underneath a tarp, located behind the back stairs. How they missed him, I will never know, but I cannot tell you how relieved I was when he was spotted.

The time had come to stop the insanity before someone got killed. Jim's desperate attempts to enter the flat, proved to the Officers that they were dealing with a dangerous, and irrational individual. Hearing the scuffle below, I could not help but think that my husband was acting like a rabid animal, as they carted him off to jail.

I have no idea as to how long he was in jail for, or what transpired, but I remember calling my mother and asking her if Jimmy and I could go stay with her. I had to get out.

* * * * * * *

For many reasons, it was decided that Jimmy and I, were safest at my mother's. Her schedule as an Evening Nursing Supervisor meant that she would be home with us during the night, and in the mornings. She also wanted to help save me money by helping care for Jimmy, on her days off.

I cannot impress upon my readers, as to how much of a difference it was to be out of that flat. It felt as though a heavy weight had been lifted from my shoulders. Even our cat Pooh, had stopped trying to escape, and settled right in to his new home. He seemed much more perky and returned to his former, sociable self.

Another change that came about was Jim began staying at the flat in Watervliet. Feeling that it was a critical mistake for my husband to be at 207, there was little that I could do; he was on his own.

I recall that things seemed to quiet down for a brief period of time, after I had left the flat. Jim had become somewhat more receptive to the supervised visitation. On some days, he was allowed to take Jimmy on prearranged visits to Jerry's, providing that he was not alone. As for any other time, he had to schedule the visit in advance, with my mother, and would come to her house.

After a few weeks of those arrangements, it appeared that

we were all making adjustments, although Jim still had moments where he would transition into a devilish guise. Most of those times involved rude comments and intimidating glares, but he refrained from violence. Reporting to a Probation Officer made him clean up his act only enough, to make life tolerable.

My mother had always been an inspiration in my life. Suffering some extremely serious health problems inclusive of cancer, and succumbing to vocal cord paralysis during thyroid surgery, she had managed to overcome incredible odds.

Given her Last Rites on the operating table when I was just a child of seven, or so, I remember my aunt walking into the waiting area, crying with the news that my mother's life was touch and go. I also remember how hard my aunt prayed that day. Even then, I could tell how profound and reaching, the power of prayer could be.

With a will tougher than nails, my mother rallied, showing us all how incredible and indestructible the human spirit could be. After years of rehabilitation and additional surgery to try and repair her vocal cords, she was able to live without a tracheostomy and had regained *some* of her voice.

Having been told by the physicians that her nursing career was over, she exceeded everyone's expectations, by not only going back to work, but being able to attain such respectful, and responsible positions as Hospital Supervisor and later, Assistant Director of Nursing.

My mother exemplified (and still does), courage and strength. If she could get through such difficulties and overcome a handicap, I knew that I could get through this sad ordeal with Jim. As would be expected, my mother's commitment to her profession, and family, was admirable.

I recall the time that she was driving back to Albany from Fort Ann, when she came upon a young man laying in the middle of the road, unresponsive from a motorcycle accident. Pulling over, she attempted to summon the attention of other motorists, who were passing by.

Finally able to send for help, she assessed the accident

victim, and determined that he needed an airway. One of the motorists whom had stopped, happened to have one in his medical kit, but did not know how to use it. Without hesitation, my mother relied on her education and skill, to insert the airway into the young man. Doing what she could with very limited means, she continued to stay with the accident victim until the police and rescue squad arrived. They advised that had it not been for her quick thinking and nursing experience, he would have died.

She has often downplayed her bravery and compassion, stating that she did it to help. She also stated that she could not stand the thought of leaving him alone; he was someone's son and would not want her own child to be left along the roadside, struggling for his life. That is my mother: One of the most compassionate human beings I know.

Managing a large group of nurses and hospital staff is no easy task, but she always made sure to celebrate someone's birthday, or a holiday, in order to boost morale. The same applies to her neighbors: Mom is there for them whether to lend a sweater for warmth, or an ear to listen to. In my mother's opinion, everyone deserves to be treated with respect and dignity; she is a Living Angel.

As my mother embarked upon a new phase of her life by helping to care for little Jimmy, and opening her home to us, I was faced with extenuating circumstances relative to my in-laws. I could not ignore the knowledge that I had gained.

The information that Jim had shared with me on the day of his 'breakdown' was extremely disturbing. I could not disregard the fact that I had to begin reducing the amount of time that Jimmy spent with them, more so, eliminating his time with them alone.

Jim did understand my concerns, but remained somewhat neutral. I remember him telling me that he did not want Jimmy to go through what he had. I was going to keep my promise to him to stop history from repeating itself, even if it meant making some uncomfortable changes.

Without a job, Jim had submitted an application to work at

Jerry's employer. As it turned out, they had called him in for an interview, and had given him a position within the manufacturing company. Due to our separation, I cannot recall exactly what his position was, but I believe he was working in a warehouse, loading trucks in Watervliet.

With an improved job situation, I was hopeful that things were going to turn around for my husband. Having to report to his Probation Officer, and prove himself responsible, looked as if it had little impact though, as at some point after going to stay with my mother, our car had vanished. I later found out that he had taken it to a friend's house.

Since the car was in his name, there was little that I could do, as I was once again forced to carpool with my mother and Carol. If he chose to drive the car at this point, he was playing with fire. Come what may, I had to accept the fact that no matter how hard he said that he was trying, his actions were speaking louder than his words.

During this timeframe, I had to make a few unpleasant trips back and forth to the flat with my mother, in order to get the last of both Jimmy and my personal items. Ugh, how I loathed even the thought having to go there.

The haze remained, and I could see that Jim was living the life of a bachelor. Nothing seemed out of the ordinary structurally, but I do vividly recall the air seemed the most intense it had ever been.

It was odd. As soon as I walked into that house, no matter how many times before, I could not shake the repressive atmosphere. It was not only powerful; it was foreboding. I also had another unusual sensation occur while making my final stop at 207, that day.

Conducting one last check to see if there was anything else that needed to be taken back to my mother's, I had walked from the nursery, through the kitchen, into the dining room and towards the entrance of the flat. Looking into the living room, I felt a sudden shift in the energy; the male spirit energy had manifested with an air of superiority.

Disturbed, I remember thinking that whoever he was, he

would not get the best of me; I was leaving 207, and had no intentions of ever going back. What items that were left, were Jim's, and would be up to him to remove when the time had come.

I remember being thankful to leave those damned energies behind, as I walked out the door, and onto 19th Street. I also could not help but feel as though I was narrowly escaping the evil grasp of a hideous monster. My son and I were not going to become a food source for the percolating vortex of negativity, and destruction. As it were, the energies had already fed off of my family and I, for just short of one year, managing to make my husband their main meal.

Letting out a sigh of relief to know that I would not have to tread foot in that place again, I got into the car and drove over to Troy. It was what I *thought* to be the end of a very bizarre chapter in my life.

Living with my mother was just what Jimmy and I needed. A good deal of hurt and fear was replaced with joy, and healing. I was coming to terms that if Jim and I did divorce, it was truly for the best. One of us had to make sure that we would be sound of mind for Jimmy. If I had to do it alone, well, then fine: Jimmy needed me and that was all that mattered.

My mother was also enjoying the companionship and loved being able to watch Jimmy grow. He was just starting to speak simple sentences and liked to listen to music, and dance in his walker, or chair. Considering everything that we had been going through, he was a very happy baby.

Busy with work and having to carpool did not come without its challenges, but they were nothing in contrast to life at 207. I was blessed to have my mother helping out, and Sarah continued to care for Jimmy on my mother's days at the facility. Planned in advance, we all had to take into consideration Jim's visitation schedule, ensuring that he would have quality time with our son.

The visits remained uneventful, other than an occasional inquisition by Jim, as to what I was doing, where I was going and whom I was hanging around with. My answers never changed, as I rarely went anywhere, had a small circle of friends and was most importantly, concentrating on Jimmy, and my job.

It was late June when I had come home from work and received a telephone call from my husband's Probation Officer. Contacting me for information relative to Jim, he asked me a series of questions that I had little, if any answers to. Unable to disclose any specific information, I was under the impression that Jim had gotten into some type of trouble.

Calling a mutual friend, I asked some questions relative their knowledge of what Jim had been doing. All they offered was that he was working with Jerry, at his new job in Watervliet. I also had learned that he was interested in a friend's 'lady neighbor,' and had been seen out with her a few times. The friend further advised me that the woman was a known drug user.

Between the call from the Probation Officer, and the information about the woman, it was clear that he was up to the same shenanigans. As hurt as I was, I had my very own "come to Jesus moment," and knew that a divorce was immanent.

10

June 28th

June 28th, 1989 began as a typical day. Jimmy and I were up early; Mom visited with us briefly as we ate our breakfast, and I finished getting ready for work. I remember the weather was sunny, hot and humid. It was also a visitation day for Jim, scheduled to take place at my mother's apartment in Troy.

My mother had the day off and would be caring for Jimmy. In addition to that, Sarah and Len had started their summer vacation, and Sarah's sister Becky, was filling in for the interim.

Carol and I had briefly talked about heading up to Maine with Karen and Jimmy, to do some relaxing for a long weekend, but nothing had been set in stone. For the most part, this was the main topic of our discussion on the way home from work that evening.

I recall not having been home for more than ten minutes, when Jim had called and asked if it was still okay for him to come over. Confirming the plans, I noticed that he seemed slightly irritated, but otherwise fine.

Just shy of dinner, Jim arrived with two large paper bags filled with gifts for Jimmy. Rather standoffish, he then advised

me that he wanted Jimmy to wait and open the gifts after
dinner. Asking where to place them, I pointed to the dresser in
my bedroom.

Jim played with Jimmy, as my mother and I prepared dinner.
We could both see that he was bothered and agreed that it was
probably associated with the phone call that his Probation
Officer had placed to me a few days before.

He was calm during dinner; not wanting to stir the pot, we
kept the conversation very simple. I do remember thinking that
it was odd that he did not eat as much as he usually would.

As we were finishing with the meal, Jim nonchalantly stated
that he was in *trouble*. My mother and I looked at one another,
waiting for him to continue. I remember him being very vague
about the details.

Trying to better understand what was going on, I did ask if
he had violated his probation. He grew very restless with my
question and did not answer me.

In an attempt to change the conversation, and void the
answer altogether, Jim asked my mother where she had parked
her car, stating that he wanted a ride home. She refused, and
offered to give him money to take a cab, or bus, back to a
friend's house, or to the flat in Watervliet.

That actually prompted an unusual remark relative to how
he felt about living in the flat by himself. Jim went on to state
how much he loved staying at 207, which completely surprised
me, given how many times he told me that he hated it. His eyes
seemed to sparkle, as though he was amused by my reaction of
disgust.

Getting up from the table, Jim's demeanor changed in an
instant. He said that he felt very tired and wanted to take a
short nap before leaving. With time constraints being set on
visitation, my mother and I were reluctant to let him lay down,
but obliged. My mother told him that under no circumstances
was he staying any later than normal.

Never one to take a nap, I remember being very surprised
by his request and more so, since he didn't want to spend the
rest of his time visiting Jimmy. In turn, I told him that he could

use my room. He then asked me to wake him up in an hour. It was already close to 7:00PM.

As Jim slept, my mother and I quietly conversed in the living room and played with Jimmy. The hour was just about over when I put Jimmy back into his highchair for a snack, before he opened up the gifts.

Entering the bedroom, I found Jim lying on his back with a pillow over his head, sprawled out diagonally, across the bed. It did not take me long to wake him up. Tossing the pillow to the side, he continued to lie there, staring at me, like he was deep in thought, or even in a waking dream; he appeared to be confused.

By then, my mother had gone back into the kitchen and started washing the dinner dishes. Reminding him that he needed to give Jimmy his gifts, I left the bedroom and told Jim that I was going to get him the cab fare and would meet him in the dining room. I remember hearing Jim get up, and then begin to rummage through the paper bags.

Placing the money on the table, I proceeded over to Jimmy, telling him that we were going to open some toys. I also recall that it seemed as though Jim was taking an awful long time to grab the gifts, and come to the room.

With my back to the kitchen as well as my bedroom, I lifted Jimmy out of the high chair, turned around and found Jim standing behind me, pointing his grandfather's shotgun at the two of us! I will never, ever forget the look in his eyes. My husband was absent in spirit, his body and soul taken over by the Devil, himself.

His voice was different and his speech pattern was unusual; he was seething mad, ranting that he was going to kill my son and I, and then himself. Stunned and cornered, I began to cry and beg for our lives. He then cruelly mocked me, repeating everything that I was saying back to me, in a very sick tone.

Inch by inch, he backed Jimmy and I farther into the corner, as he continued his threats describing in detail what he was going to do to us. I pleaded for him to stop, and begged for him to spare Jimmy's life, and take mine.

Alerted to the situation after turning off the water at the sink, my mother could hear that we were in peril. I will also never forget the look on her face, as she emerged from the kitchen to find Jimmy and I, backed into the far corner, at the mercy of a gun-wielding monster.

Slowly, she started to move closer to Jim's side, asking him very calmly, to put the gun down. Unflinching, he kept the weapon aimed at Jimmy and I. I recall thinking that I was going to see my son *and* my dear mother killed before my very eyes, as he stated that he was going to shoot me last, and then him self. Weeping and shaking, I held onto Jimmy and prayed, as my very brave mother strategically maneuvered towards us.

There was no more than two and a half feet between the muzzle of the gun, and my chest. I could not imagine what my mother was trying to do as she tried to talk him out of his plans, using negotiating skills she had learned in nursing.

As he continued to lash-out, she overtly positioned herself in the open space between the gun and my chest, creating a human shield. Soon, she was face-to-face with Jim, with her back turned towards my son and I. She was trying to protect us.

I kept crying and looking at my son, his big green eyes wide with fear; this was so unfair to him. He knew that something very bad was happening, and was witnessing his father lose his mind. I have *never* felt so helpless. All I wanted to do was protect him.

"Please, dear God, please!" I prayed out loud. "Please let Jimmy go! Please let him live!" I cried. Scared to death, I was shaking so hard that I thought I was going to pass out.

My mother continued to use emotion as a method to reach him. We think that it was close to four minutes of her speaking to him, when by divine intervention, his facial expression changed and his body became somewhat relaxed, as though someone had flipped a switch. It was surreal: The look on his face went from homicidal, to having no idea what he had been doing.

For that fleeting moment my mother was able to make contact with him, he lowered the gun, stared at us for a few seconds, turned and ran out the door like a wounded animal, with the shotgun in his hand.

My mother immediately ran towards the door, locked it and began barricading it with furniture, as I called the Troy Police Department, completely panic-stricken. My mother then moved to the rear of the apartment and began to push furniture in front of the back door. Conveying the details to the Dispatch Officer was difficult; I would not let my mother take Jimmy from me – I had to hold on to him.

Since Jim had left brandishing a shotgun, the response time of the police was immediate. I could hear sirens approach, as Dispatch remained on the line until the first Officers entered the apartment.

Several of the Troy Police Department's finest, had arrived on-scene with cars positioned both to the front and back of the house. In an attempt to calm me down long enough to give them details, my mother finally took Jimmy from my arms, as I explained what had transpired.

By now, they had the back of the house secured, with Officers staked-out in the alley, in the house, and outside the front of the building. Scouring the city of Troy, were several patrol cars responding to an APB that had been issued by the Troy P.D. Since Jim had left on foot, it was very difficult to detect where he may have gone. Just about one mile over the Congress Street Bridge from Troy was the flat at 207, but there were no reports of his surfacing in Albany County.

I remember the Officers also asking me what friends, bars, establishments, and restaurants Jim may have frequented, but not knowing the names of most, I could only best describe them by location. For the most part, I was clueless.

Sending up a squad car to check out one of the bars on upper Congress Street, a patron, or Bartender, had stated seeing Jim come in, noting that he had left before the police had arrived. The fact that the party did not notice a gun meant very little, as they were under the impression that he had probably disassembled it, and had found something to carry the parts in.

Pouring over the city for close to an hour and a half without any other sightings, the police then escorted me to a patrol car, to help search the neighborhood for any possible signs of my husband. It seemed as though he had evaporated into thin air, after stopping at the bar.

Stressed and uneasy that their search came up empty-handed, I remember questioning them if it was going to be safe for us to stay at my mother's apartment. Nobody seemed to have answers – only more questions.

With several police agencies in both Rensselaer, and Albany counties on the lookout, Jim had been able to evade the law. My anxiety grew, as I began to fear the worst.

I believe that it was close to two hours after the incident, when police decided to cut back on their presence outside of the house, leaving one Officer to patrol the perimeter, while one remained inside, with the three of us. I remember that it was around 10:00PM when I received a bone-chilling phone call.

A mutual friend called my mother's apartment and asked me if I knew where Jim was. Not wanting to go into detail about what had transpired, and the police unsure if individual may be scouting information for Jim, I responded by asking them, "*Why?*" With their voice raised in alarm, the individual stated that Jim had just called their house, and had asked them to pass along the following message:

"Tell Jill, Jimmy and everyone else, that I love them. It's over." He then hung up the phone.

Teetering on the brink of alarm, I relayed the information to the Officer stationed inside of our apartment. The friend began to lose control and hung up the phone. It was a haunting message that would foretell a tragic outcome.

In response to the call, the Officer radioed the information through the appropriate channels. We didn't know what was going to happen.

Time seemed to come to a standstill. I was sick with worry, as was my mother. Keeping her cool, she spoke with the Officer as I racked my brain, trying to think of where he could have gone.

I cannot remember how much time had passed but I am going to say that it was close to 11:15PM when the Officer inside of our apartment received a call from the station. Hearing only his side of the conversation, both my mother and I noted his tone and demeanor: He had been given some type of information; however, did not convey what it was. Ending the call, he appeared quite solemn, almost like he wanted to say something to us – but for whatever the reason, chose not to.

Our home telephone rang a few minutes later; it was an Officer from the Watervliet Police Department. They had called to advise me that they had found my husband. Stating that they did not have any additional information at the time, they then asked to speak with my mother.

Immediately, I had noticed a change in my mother's voice. For the life of me, I recall being unable to understand why they had wanted to speak to her, and why her answers became single-worded. She hung up the phone and looked at me with a blank expression, and then asked to speak with the Officer in the kitchen.

When my mother came back into the living room, she had tears in her eyes. I remember begging her to tell me what was wrong. Neither she, nor the Officer would tell me a thing, other than they had found Jim.

Every time that I would ask if he was O.K., my mother and the Officer would tell me that the Watervliet P.D. was trying to "figure things out." The less they would tell me, the more I knew that they were keeping something from me. Growing more impatient and distressed by the moment, I decided to call the Watervliet Police Department, requesting that they answer my questions.

I remember being put on hold, only to have Dispatch pick back up, and ask to speak with my mother again. Taking the phone from my hand, my mother again, went back to speaking yes-no answers. A few moments later, she thanked the Dispatch Officer, and then hung up the phone.

Kneeling down next to me with tears in her eyes, she took my hand and said, "Oh, honey. I'm so sorry to have to tell you this…Jim is dead. He shot himself."

In that instant, my entire life turned upside down. I just barely remember the Troy Police Officer telling me that he was sorry. I vaguely remember him stating me how incredibly fortunate we were all to be alive. He then informed us that two Detectives from the Watervliet Police Department were going to come over to speak with my mother and I, about the incident. He left a short while afterwards.

I could not fathom, nor understand, what had transpired. I was having a hard enough time trying to process what occurred after dinner before Jim had left, let alone what, where and how, he had killed himself.

Balling my eyes out, I recall running into Jimmy's room, where I found him awake in his crib. I just wanted to hold him and tell him how much I loved him – and how much his daddy loved him.

Sobbing uncontrollably, I picked him up, with my mother looking-on in the doorway. I remember Jimmy said, "Mama? Dada? Mama? Dada?" He *knew* something was wrong.

My mother came over to comfort us, as she and I huddled around little Jimmy, and cried. Noticing that I was on the verge of passing out, my mother took Jimmy from my arms, as I stumbled towards a chair and collapsed. I was devastated.

I really cannot remember who called Carol, but I recall her rushing to our apartment. Understandably shocked by the horrible news, she wanted to let us know that she was there for us. Upset herself, she had been driving too fast, and had been pulled over by a policeman while en route. Fortunately for Carol, the Officer had been aware of the manhunt, and upon learning where she was headed, issued her a warning, and let her go.

I do recall that I was exhausted by the time the two Watervliet Detectives finally arrived. Stating their condolences, they said that it was routine to have to conduct an interview, in order to process the case. For as many questions that they asked of me, I seemed to ask many more. Their body language and expressions said it all; it was a bad, bad scene.

What I do remember learning, was that Jim had eventually made his way from Troy, back to Watervliet. He had also purchased some beer, and had gone back to 207 19th Street. Nobody is entirely sure how long he had been there, when he made the decision to leave the flat, and walk across the street to use the telephone at the Pizza Parlor. That was the location where Jim had placed the call to our friend, stating the last words that anyone would ever hear him speak.

One of the Owner's family members had overheard Jim's conversation on the phone, and thought it was unusual. He then walked back across the street to 207, and within a few very brief minutes, an explosion rang out from the house.

The woman who had overheard the conversation connected the sound with what was said, and became hysterical. Someone from the Pizza Parlor contacted the police.

Vinny, who lived in the first floor flat, was rattled by the noise and vibration. If my memory serves me correctly, he had stated that he thought a truck had blown a tire in front of the house, on 19th Street. He apparently went outside to inspect the noise, and then called the police for further investigation.

Evidently, the Watervliet P.D. had also been looking for Jim in conjunction with what had occurred at my mother's house in Troy. Unable to find him, it was upon receipt of the call from the Pizza Parlor, along with Vinny's, that they realized what was going on.

It was not until the police arrived, that Vinny was questioned, and then later asked to identify my husband's body. He had died from a self-inflicted, .12 gauge gunshot wound to the head, which killed him instantly: He was only identifiable by the tattoos on his arms – the antique gun at his side. We were then advised where his body was taken for autopsy, and told that toxicology tests had been ordered as standard protocol, given his suicide.

Some details surrounding Jim's death are extremely personal. Due to the graphic nature and manner, I am not compelled to discuss the information. The only thing that I will say, is that according to the Detectives, other Officers, along with my first floor neighbor, it was a horrifying scene that adversely impacted several of those present on-scene that night.

With all of this information at hand, I had one question that nobody wanted to answer: How did Jim get the shotgun back from the police station? No matter how many times I would ask, they redirected my inquiry, advising me to call the station in the morning.

Of little consolation, I remember telling them that someone needed to be ashamed of them selves for giving back his gun. Yes, perhaps he may have found another weapon, but the fact that it had been taken by the police for safekeeping, and then given back to someone on probation, facing major jail time, who was at times suicidal, was mind boggling.

Repeatedly, the Detectives remarked how blessed we were to be alive, and that even as despondent as Jim may have been, something my mother had said connected with him, long enough for him to leave. Overwhelmed by his death, it was a miracle he spared us, thanks to my mother's quick thinking and God's grace.

In shock, I remember crying for what seemed like forever. The next morning, I had to slowly begin to break the tragic news of Jim's death. Of little help, I could only relay the information that the Detectives had given me. I also remember thinking; how could life be so cruel?

Knowing that Sarah and Len were out of state on summer vacation, I had to go to Sarah's sister's house, and tell her what had happened. At this point, I remember feeling *numb*.

I also remember trying to find out who had given Jim the gun. Not wanting to go into the police station directly, I called that afternoon, demanding an explanation: Not one person could offer me reasonable cause.

At first, I was first told that one of Jim's friends came in to the station and claimed it was his antique shotgun, stating that he let Jim borrow it, and wanted it back. I was later told they had no idea how it was released.

To this day, I still do not know how he got his hands on it, but do know that someone made an error in judgment, while others may have been playing a game called C.Y.A. It still upsets me to think about this aspect, and I often wonder if the parties involved, felt badly when they had learned of Jim's death.

Regardless of who gave him the gun, or how it ended up in Jim's hands that night, the fact remains that the outcome could not be changed – the damage was done. Painfully evident was the fact, that my husband, unable to stave-off the literal and figurative demons that had plagued his mind and soul, had succumbed to the pressure. Equally as atrocious, the dark forces that cruelly tormented him for almost one year had unjustly claimed the life of the man I loved.

11

Oppression & Possession

I do not know what I would have done without the help of my family and close friends. For all of them, I am forever thankful and truly appreciate every ounce of support and love they gave Jimmy and I. Once Becky had notified Len and Sarah of Jim's death, they broke-off the remainder of their vacation, and headed back to New York.

Tensions were somewhat high surrounding my in-laws. Ever since Jim had confided in me about his childhood, I had been limiting the time that Jimmy and I would visit. Additionally, I no longer had allowed Jimmy to be in their house, without my being present. Having discussed the issues at hand with my mother-in-law, she did understand, but was still upset with the restrictions. I might add that it is not a matter of public knowledge to discuss what my husband disclosed, as that remains a very private matter.

My family and friends helped guide me through planning Jim's services; most of which remains a blur. I remember sitting in the funeral home feeling overwhelmed with details. We wanted Jim to receive a proper burial, and give everyone the opportunity to show their respects, but were limited to what we could and could not do, from the perspective of a viewing.

Due to the autopsy, Jim's services were pushed back a day. I remember that initially, there was some concern that it was so close to the Fourth of July holiday, that we would have wait until afterwards. Thankfully, the Coroner was able to finish his work rather swiftly. Jim's interment was scheduled for July 3rd.

The day of my husband's wake was unbelievably draining. I remember everyone telling me that the hardest was yet to come: The day of his funeral. I could not imagine how anything could be even more difficult than the wake, but sadly, would later understand what they had meant.

Due to the nature and manner of Jim's death, a request had been made for security to be present at both the wake and funeral. Not initially understanding this, it was not until a few days later, would I realize the importance of the request; a handful of people were exhibiting irrational behavior.

Another issue that had been addressed was the fact that I could not give Jim an open-casket viewing. Additionally, I had been advised that his casket would be locked and turned, in the event that anyone should become curious. Much to my horror, a mourner did try to open it during the service, but was pulled back by a member of security, unable to succeed.

People seemed to come out of the woodwork, to pay their respects to my husband. Most of them I knew, but some I did not. They all recalled his life with affection. With respect to his setbacks and life struggles, everyone remembered what a good-hearted, funny man he was. I recall wondering how I would ever recover – how, and why this nightmare even happened.

A rather extraordinary event occurred during the last hour of the wake, when Father came to say a blessing for Jim. Close family and friends had gathered in the Viewing Room to pay their respects. I remember sitting in between my mother and grandmother. Diagonal to me on the other side of the room, was Jim's family. As Father prayed, I remember staring at his back, listening to his every word, praying with all of my heart. I wanted Jim to know that I forgave him and asked that God would guide him, to rest in peace.

While praying with my eyes facing downward, something caught my attention: On the floor next to Father's shoes, appeared a gold light, the size of a softball. Slowly, it rose up Father's back and stopped over the casket. I thought I was seeing things and remembering trying to refocus my swollen, irritated eyes. After blinking several times, the faint globe remained hovering above Jim's coffin.

Looking towards the golden light, I felt a great deal of energy reflecting off of Father. Deep in prayer, there came an intense heat that filled the room; it was incredible. Within minutes of its appearance, and just before he concluded the service, I remember seeing the light rise upwards towards the ceiling and then disappear. I did not say a word to anyone about it, until after going home and asking my grandmother and mother if they had noticed anything.

Although they had not seen the light, they did notice the sudden and dramatic temperature change that came from out of nowhere during the prayer service. I sensed, as did my mother and grandmother, that it was an Angel, coming to help Jim cross. After all that he had been through, I considered that a comforting sign.

The morning of the funeral was excruciatingly difficult for me. I wanted to cling to Jimmy, but knew that he was best removed from the events of the day. I will forever remember this day more than any other, as I realized how very possible it was for someone to die from a broken heart.

Upon arrival at the funeral home, we were ordered into a group of limousines dedicated to family members. While waiting for the procession to line up, I had been conversing with my sister-in-law, outside of one of the vehicles.

I remember making a remark that Father's prayer service was both beautiful, and intense. I also told her that I had noticed something very unusual.

Jerking her head up, she then exclaimed that she too, had seen something, describing it as a "glowing ball" that had come up behind Father as he knelt at Jim's side. Neither one of us could believe it; we had witnessed the same thing!

Asking her to further elaborate, she described what I had noticed, but from a different angel, given we were seated on opposite sides of the room. I recall several family members who overheard the conversation, had shared the same sentiment: An Angel came to take Jim home.

I remember the church was packed. I had again broken down and could not stop crying. Sitting to the right of Jim's casket, I kept thinking back to our wedding, Jimmy's baptism, as well as some of the Sunday services we had attended over the last three years. Who would have ever thought that just seven months after Jimmy's baptismal ceremony, that Jim would be dead? In the back of my mind, I knew that my husband had truly endured a very rough life, but I also was sure that 207 had something to do with his death – more than I could bear to think at that time.

I remember leaving the church; walking behind Jim's casket, flanked by undercover security. I also recall thinking that it was the last time Jim would pass through the doors of the church that had welcomed him since he was a very little boy. I could barely stand the pain in my heart, and truly thought it was going to be the death of me.

As we left the church and headed to the cemetery, I remember my grandmother had told me to look behind us; it was car after car, as far as the eye could see. I remember that someone had counted the cars in the procession, and was advised that it was over eighty vehicles long. It was a testimony to the fact that my husband had touched so many people's lives.

I also recall that it was incredibly warm that day, even for a morning interment. Between the heat as well as the emotional, and physical exhaustion that I was experiencing, I was somewhat woozy by the time we actually reached his plot. I remember that I had become slightly dizzy as I exited the car, and was advised by my mother to sit and wait a few minutes as the Funeral Director surrounded Jim's casket with mounds of beautiful flowers.

Approaching his graveside, surrounded by family, close friends and security, I recall dozens and dozens of people piling out of their cars and gathering around Jim, to say farewell. I also remember thinking that it would be the last time I would 'see' him. My heart felt as though it would fail, as I began to sway from lightheadedness.

As each moment ticked by, I remember trying not to pass out. It was, and still exists, one of the most painful experiences I have ever had to endure.

My memory becomes foggy trying to recall what happened at this juncture. Father had motioned for me to place my roses on the casket; all that I can remember is taking a few steps and my knees gave out, as I almost tumbled onto Jim's casket. I remember the plain clothed Security Officers grabbing me by each side, and pulling me up. There was gasping and crying, as I was escorted back to the limousine, where it was cool; my mother and grandmother arrived behind me for support. I remember that I just wanted to go home and hold my son.

* * * * * * *

I was in no frame of mind to hold any type of party. In fact, I remember dozing in and out of sleep and being forced to drink a good deal of water, due to dehydration. Much later that evening, I received a call from my mother-in-law, asking me if my grandmother, mother and I, would stop by their house for a celebration in Jim's honor.

Initially, I declined, but my grandmother felt that it would be a good idea to go for a few minutes so long as I felt up to it. She also thought it was a good gesture, given that my husband had committed suicide *on his mother's birthday.*

My mother stayed at home, as my grandmother drove me to my in-laws. I could have never been prepared for what I saw: A full-blown party was underway. Making our way through the large crowd, music blared and alcohol poured in excess. Entering the house, my mother-in-law was sitting in the living room and motioned for my grandmother and I, to go over.

Jerry approached me a short time later. I had not had an opportunity to really speak with him since Jim had passed. He had tried to counsel Jim, but admittedly had felt as though it was a useless cause; at that stage, Jim was not listening to anyone, his best friend included. I knew that Jerry was hurting though, and had to thank him for always being there for us both.

As soon as he could meander his way through the crowd, he came over and gave me a huge hug. For minutes we embraced and cried, as people looked-on. We agreed to talk privately, before my grandmother and I left to go home.

Not wanting to stay terribly long, my grandmother and I visited for a bit, and then headed out to speak with Jerry in a quiet area of the yard. He had mentioned that he needed to tell me something, but first made me promise not to "hate" him. Reassuring him that I would not, Jerry stated that he knew Jim had gotten himself into quite a mess, by which he felt partially responsible; Jim had been using cocaine.

Jerry then stated that he had caught Jim, and a lady friend, using the drug approximately a month, or so, prior to his death. Apparently, Jim had told him that it was none of his concern, and asked him to stay out of his affairs. Jerry then stated that if it was of any consolation, Jim did not use it regularly.

I could tell how sad and frustrated that he too, had become, knowing that no matter what he did, he couldn't pull his buddy out of the funk. It was so sad to see that everyone who loved my husband had felt helpless after attempting to talk sense into him.

My grandmother asked Jerry if he was aware of what plagued Jim relative to 'personal issues,' by which Jerry stated he had known about all along. I remember Jerry being somewhat shocked that Jim had not until recently, disclosed that information to me.

After our talk, my grandmother and I made our way back through the crowd and headed towards the parking lot. Walking with us, Jerry first hugged my grandmother goodbye, and then me. Finding our selves crying again, he promised that whatever Jimmy and I needed, he would always be there for us. He also assured me that Jim truly loved us all, but was "not himself when he died." I remember forcing out, "No, he was not."

Back at home with my mother, my grandmother and I, discussed the conversation that we had with Jerry. At the time, my grandmother and I were sitting on the couch, facing the mantel of my mother's fireplace, while my mother was sitting in the chair next to it, facing the two of us. We had been focused on trying to figure out what had made Jim snap.

With all three of us in agreement, we suspected that 207 had played a significant role in the demise of my husband's sanity. I also recall that during the conversation, my grandmother kept removing her glasses and wiping them clean. She did that approximately five, to six times.

Our intense conversation was interrupted by a loud *CRASH,* when an 8"x10" photo of Jim, Jimmy and I, had fallen from the mantel, smashing onto the floor. The three of us jumped with fright! The beautiful glass frame that had encased my favorite family photo had shattered into a million pieces.

Rattled by the timing and unknown cause, we sat in silence, looking at one another thinking the same thing: Something was still very wrong. No sooner had we recovered from the shock of the falling frame, than a loud *THUD,* boomed in the direction of the dining room. It was like something out of a horror movie!

My grandmother said nothing, made the sign of the cross and held on to her crucifix necklace as she prayed. That really scared my mother, and I.

Ignoring the glass on the floor, my mother walked into the dining room to check to see if she could identify the source of the noise, yet could not. I had noticed that the air had shifted and was heavy, almost identical to how it felt in 207. I could not believe it!

As my mother returned to the living room and examined the mantel to determine what had caused the photograph to fall, my grandmother recited *The Lord's Prayer*, and *Hail Mary*, several times. She was also asking for protection. After several minutes of feverish appeal, my grandmother looked up and asked me to get the telephone: She wanted the number to the rectory, so she could call Father. "Father?" my mother and I, chimed-in. "Why do you want to call *Father?*" we asked in unison.

She meant business and was not about to spend time explaining anything. Shaking, I dialed Father's number, telling him who I was. I then stated that my grandmother was requesting to speak with him. My mother and I had no clue what she was about to say. It was quite late and I was surprised that he even answered the phone.

My grandmother then went on to tell him what happened with the picture frame and loud noise. She also told him that just before the frame fell from the mantel, she saw the spirit energy of a male – not Jim – standing in front of the fireplace, something that then made sense as to why she kept removing her glasses. It wasn't to clean them; she was trying to decipher what she was seeing and wanted to make sure there was nothing on her glasses!

Continuing, she told Father that she was picking up on something "bad" and wanted him to pray for us. A few moments later, she and Father were reciting more prayers over the phone, as my mother and I listened.

Ending the discussion, my grandmother stated that she would speak to Father the next day, and hung up the phone. I remember asking her to explain what she had meant by telling Father she felt "something bad," but she refused to tell us. Worn out from Jim's funeral, and now shell-shocked by two anomalous events that had just transpired, I needed to go to bed.

The definition of "something bad" lingered in the heavy, room air. I remember very little after resting my head on my pillow, as I had passed-out cold, while praying myself to sleep.

The next day, I began to develop a horrible sinus infection from all of the crying I had been doing. I remember being exhausted and trying to find the strength to do simple tasks. I also remember the heavy feeling that had crept into the house the night before, was gone.

Considering that I had a terrible headache, I had been looking forward to Jimmy coming back home. Since the services were over, I felt that he needed to get back to his routine, and sleep in his own crib: I could not wait to see him.

I also had remembered that my grandmother was going to be speaking with Father again. Unsure as to how the day would unfold due to my raging sinus issue, I remember hoping that I would be able to listen to their conversation. I knew that if my grandmother said it was "bad," from a psychic perspective; it was *bad*.

My grandmother's intuition and clairvoyant abilities were amazing. One of the biggest predictions that she had was the John F. Kennedy assassination, in 1963. Not only did that greatly upset even her self, the ripple effect that it had relative to my grandfather, would become the basis for one of their biggest arguments.

Apparently, my grandmother had a premonition just a few days prior to John F. Kennedy's death. She recounted this dream premonition in front of my very agitated grandfather, who was trying to get out the door, and go to work. Taking it all in stride, she said he acknowledged her concern, and then took off.

The dream repeated itself the next night. Frantic about what it entailed, she told my grandfather, who stated that although she did have a history of accurate predictions, the vision was preposterous in theory. My grandmother stated that she prayed for the safety of the President and held her breath.

A day later, after learning of the assassination, my grandmother was quite understandably overwhelmed with grief, along with the rest of the nation, as well as the entire world. My grandfather was absolutely speechless. Pointing out the details of her dreams to my grandfather only made a bad situation, that much worse.

An extremely patriotic man, he had served as a Sergeant in the United States Army during WWII. He was dumbfounded with my grandmother's prediction, and admittedly spooked.

Due to the scope and magnitude of her vision, my grandfather made my grandmother promise that she would never tell him about any future premonitions. She was also told never to utter even one peep about a hunch, inkling, dream or any type of warning.

So many years later, while spending some of my summer vacation with her, my grandmother helped me to better understand that not everyone would be accepting of my abilities. Sharing personal anecdotes about her own life, as well as my great-great grandmother's relative to the world of psychic gifts, I was told to hold on to the truth, even when faced by those who would try to discredit me, or would be unable, or unwilling to understand.

Mentioning her infamous prediction about the President to me, my grandfather, who was laying on the sofa in the family room, was quick to banish us to the front porch. After all those years, he still was adamant that she was not to talk about anything psychic, or paranormal, while in his presence.

At the time of Jim's death, my grandmother was transitioning from being a devout Roman Catholic, to more open-minded, basing her spirituality on a blend of her Native American roots, and Catholicism. Given that we had frequently discussed our abilities and the familial histories of them, it was through her own personal experiences that she realized that religion and church were an extension of personal spirituality. She had taught me that through life, we all evolve as spiritual beings, using each and every event to shape our spiritual selves. My grandmother also instilled that religion was learned in a book, whereas spirituality was something that flourished from birth: Spirituality is an innate characteristic of each and every human being, which *needs* to be nurtured.

When it had come time to converse with Father that day, she actually discussed those very aspects with him, as well as the power of prayer. She had found a sense of peace, but still relied on the connection she had built after so many years of being deeply involved with the Catholic Church.

With a brief explanation to Father about her beliefs and abilities, she revealed the basis of her prior call. I remember that they were also discussing the impact of committing suicide, in relationship to a spirit's unrest.

Only privy to my grandmother's side of the conversation, I spent most of my time trying to figure out what Father was saying to her. It had become obvious that both my grandmother and Father were in agreement about the issue of suicide relative to the Catholic faith. Raised Roman Catholic myself, I knew enough about the shame placed on not only suicide victims, but also of potential attachments that they formed in the environment, at the time of death.

I cannot recall the exact turning point of their conversation, but I know that it was shortly after my grandmother asked Father if he thought that Jim's soul was at unrest. She mentioned not liking the flat at 207, she also told Father about the photo she wanted to show Jim of Pope John Paul II. I had never even picked up on that at the time, and had considered Jim's actions rude, more than anything; however, listening to my grandmother speak with Father, brought something completely unexpected to the table.

She then asked Father if Jim could have been *possessed*. It was shortly thereafter that my mother blessed herself and folded her hands in prayer. Never having even considered a possession, or having known of any actual phenomenon having occurred, I remember being totally freaked out by her suggestion.

After the lengthy call, my grandmother once more thanked Father for his time and insight, and ended the discussion. She then asked my mother for some holy water, as she was instructed by Father to sprinkle it throughout the house and recite prayer.

Without questioning her, my mother got up to fetch my grandmother a small bottle. She then proceeded to bless my mother's apartment, making sure to cast-out any dark, or evil forces. She also prayed that Jim's spirit would rest in peace.

Following the blessing, my grandmother discussed the details of her conversation with Father, which primarily focused on Father's suspicion that due to Jim's alcohol and substance abuse issues, as well as other issues, the environment in the flat could have been one that facilitated an oppression and or, possession.

I remember thinking that the entire situation made sense, yet seemed like something written from a Stephen King novel. It was so bizarre and surreal, that I had wished I could just close 'the book,' and put it away for good. Sadly, it was a very real, and apparently possible, scenario.

Hoping and praying that the blessing would rid the house of whatever came in the night prior, I began to ask my grandmother questions about the energies in 207. She then explained that on a few occasions in her past, she had experienced something evil and had to sage smudge it out, or bless it with holy water.

She also stated that due to my experiences being somewhat limited due to my age, that I was unable to discern what was actually going on. Additionally, my grandmother mentioned it was also entirely possible that the energy was disguising itself and not presenting itself in a direct manner, in order to take control of anything – anyone – that it could.

My grandmother continued to explain that with oppressions and possessions, the weakest link tends to suffer. Due to Jim's issues with at least drinking, in addition to the personal experiences that shaped his emotional state from childhood, he was an unsuspecting, and unfortunate candidate for that to happen.

She also stated that some people have a difficult time understanding and believing that an oppression and possession can occur. Given the Catholic religion, and their views of demonic oppression and possession, in addition to her abilities, she had been very well aware of those forces for many years.

Perhaps Jim had fallen victim to an oppression and possession, but if that was the case, how were the energies in 207, going to be rid of? Was Jim the first person to die in the flat? I could not help but think, that he was not.

The energy of that creepy old man in black, which had

appeared in front of our tree on Christmas Eve and manifested itself a few times afterwards, seemed to be controlled by a more concentrated evil power. I remember asking my grandmother if it could have traveled across the bridge to my mother's. Unsure of the culprit, she was confident that she had been able to cast-out whatever had infiltrated my mother's, when she conducted the blessing.

Whether by blessing, prayer, or the combination of both, the energy never penetrated my mother's house again. Though the causes of the frame crashing to the ground, and the loud boom heard in the dining room had never been discovered, the three of us, including Father, agreed that it had something to do with spirit energy, if not from Jim, from 207, directly.

* * * * * * *

At this point, any thought of 207 made me ill. The issues beforehand seemed like an atrocious series of warnings that would be forever embedded in memory. I found it extremely difficult to consider making a trip back there, to pick up Jim's mementos. I also had to wait until our Landlord was finished cleaning the living room, where Jim had died.

Once my bereavement leave was up and I had recovered from a short hospitalization for a sinus infection, I changed my status at the hospital to part time. I will never forget the phone call that I received at work, on my first day back to the office.

It was late in the morning, when my Landlord in Watervliet had called. Anticipating his phone call much earlier, he stated that he didn't want to intrude so close to Jim's passing. He had always been a very kind man, and I could sense his sincerity during our conversation.

Immediately offering his condolences, he was devastated by the turn of events. I could hear the sadness in his voice as it cracked, and he fought back tears. He then asked what I was going to do with Jim's items that remained in the flat. I told him that I would try to get there as soon as I could, in order to pick up keepsakes, and that I would have his close friends take care of the rest. Continuing to express his sympathy I still remember how compassionate he was, while speaking with me.

Expressing how upset he was to have to see my family and I go through such a tragedy, he told me that he could not believe "this was happening again." *Happening again?* What exactly did he mean by, *"happening again?"*

He then continued to state that at some point several years prior, either while a family member had owned the house, or just prior to the relative buying it, one of the Tenants at 207 had committed suicide in the *same room* as Jim. He did state that it was a male who had shot himself, but he was confused as to when. He mentioned the early 1960's, but had a difficult time recollecting the specific year.

My Landlord was stupefied to find out someone else had died in the same manner, happening twice within a few decades. I cannot tell you who was more shocked: My Landlord, finding out *another* person had committed suicide in the house, or me, to learn that there had been a past death in the same room of the flat. We both agreed that it was quite an *unusual* coincidence.

With this information, I began to put together the pieces of the strange and tragic puzzle called *207*. As much as I hated to consider it, the possession issue then began to make even more, horrifying sense. My mother and grandmother were equally taken back by the news. Unfortunately, the fact remained that I had to make one last trip to the flat, and pack up some of Jim's things. The new information made a distressing situation, even more so.

I believe it was the weekend following my conversation with my Landlord, when my mother and I drove to Watervliet. With instructions to bless our selves upon entering 207, my mother and I anxiously drove across the Congress Street Bridge in silence; the red brick house, a very visible beacon of terror.

I knew that our Landlord had made an attempt to clean the living room of the flat as to remove any evidence of what had happened, but I had been forewarned that there was a hole in the wall from the gunshot blast.

Extremely nauseated, I remember pulling up to the curb in front of the house. As my mother and I exited the car, we blessed ourselves, and asked God for protection. I also practiced the intentional 'blocking' method that my grandmother had taught me.

I remember that upon entering the flat, the haze seemed very heavy, but super-charged; it was very weird. I recall my mother and I, both noticing the peculiar change. It was almost like the energies had gained incredible strength. I look back and can almost sense it today – it was tremendously powerful – almost electric.

As I walked in the direction of nursery, my mother had stopped in the archway of the living room, performing a cursory search of the room. Trying to muster enough courage to go into the living room to see if there were any items that I needed to pack, I remember feeling my legs shake with every step, as I intentionally left that location for the last place to check.

Making my way back towards the front of the house, I stopped in the master bedroom and remember seeing my mother slowly move into the front living room area, silently looking up at the ceiling, and in the direction of the fireplace, while blessing her self. Neither of us spoke; the silence was deafening.

It was after I had gone into the master bedroom when I began to notice a very faint, yet sickening odor that was coming from the living room. The open windows seemed to make it more pronounced, as it was carried along the light breeze. I had always been told that the smell of death was something one would never forget, and I could then identify why: It was *disgusting*.

I remember calling out to my mother and asking her why the scent lingered if they had cleaned. Quietly, she muttered, "Just horrible."

Approaching the nightstand that was on Jim's side of the bed, I noticed a small photo of my family. I recall picking up the wallet-sized picture and bursting into tears. "Why? Why?

Why?" I sobbed, my stomach tied in knots, and my chest heavy with indescribable grief.

Hearing me cry, my mother asked if I was going to be all right. Stumbling through the tears, I tried to regain my composure. Praying for strength to confront the scene of my husband's suicide, I put the photograph back on the nightstand, and walked into the living room, choking back my tears.

Just to the right of the fireplace, my mother was hunched over, looking at something underneath the window. She turned her head towards me, pointing to a large hole just below the ledge of the sill.

The first thing that struck me was the amount of damage it must have done upon impact, to create a hole like that, after exiting Jim's body. The second thing that crossed my mind was the memory of having our Christmas tree in that very corner, and the appearance of the male energy in that exact area; it sent chills throughout my entire body.

Overcome with emotion, I had just turned around to leave the room when I felt something become lodged in the sole of my tennis shoe. It felt like a rock.

I remember trying to scrape the object free but it wouldn't budge; it was stuck in the rubber of the sole. Stabilizing myself against the west wall, I lifted my foot to pull out the object, only to find a quarter-sized piece of bone fragment.

Throwing it on the floor, I completely lost control of my emotions. My mother, who had come to my aid to see what had happened, picked up the object and was instantaneously mortified, throwing the bone back onto the floor. In an effort to console me, she tried to give me a hug, but I knew that I had to leave the flat: I couldn't take it any more.

Hysterical, I broke away from her and upon leaving the living room, noticed a tremendous amount of blood splatter still covering the ceiling, quite a distance away from the original impact. I had also noticed a few more small pieces of skull and hair fragments against the north wall. I ran empty-handed, down the stairs and back to the car, trying not to vomit. I did not want anything from that flat – nothing at all.

My mother followed, leaving the key in the door, as instructed. Due to the graphic nature of what was overlooked in the preliminary cleaning process, she would later state that even she her self, was not prepared for what she saw.

Unable to drive, I rolled up into the fetal position on the passenger's side of the car. I had felt as though someone had punched me in the gut with such ferocity, that I could not breathe. Traumatized, I knew that I would never go back to 207; it was a House of Horrors.

A few days later, Len and Jerry met at 207, and took what they wanted. They too, commented on the hole in the wall, as well as some of the remains that had been overlooked.

Len was very bothered. Jerry acted as though he was having a difficult time processing what he had seen. Neither could believe that this was the second time a man had committed suicide in that very room. It was almost *too* strange.

Questions slowly began to surface within our social circle as to if this was more than just a coincidence, especially after learning of the house's history. What else had happened at 207? Could the other man who died, have endured what Jim had?

Whatever the origin of the entities, they had impacted several people's lives, and unfortunately, it wasn't too long after Jim's death, that someone else had an unexpected paranormal experience relative to 207. It just would not quit.

A very close friend of Jim's had been driving through Watervliet with their daughter, en route to Latham. They were stopped at the light on the corners of 19th Street and 2nd Avenue, facing north, towards 207. Looking up into the well-lit flat, Jim's friend made a remark to the effect that Jim was painting. The daughter, concerned that her mother had momentarily forgotten that Jim had just passed away, looked at her and followed the direction of her stare. Sure enough, she herself saw what they believed was Jim's silhouette, standing in the window, holding a paint roller. When they turned left at the light to head west on 19th Street, his silhouette was gone.

After gaining my composure, I asked which of the two windows they saw him in. They stated the left (facing the building from the street). They were still quite upset from the ordeal, and also had no idea that Carol and I saw a silhouette in that same window, months beforehand. I then explained that very experience, to them.

Confounded by the fact that we had similar experiences, the friend, a devout Roman Catholic, actually contacted my Landlord to see if anyone had been painting in the flat that night. He advised her that nobody had been there to repaint at that point, and was bothered that she and her daughter insisted someone was there. It was another random apparition.

Several weeks after Jim's death, I received the toxicology report from the Coroner's Office. It had detailed the gruesome cause of Jim's death, and also revealed he had an elevated B.A.C. (Blood Alcohol Content). It *did not* find any evidence of drugs. I was baffled by the absence of drugs in Jim's system, relative to Jerry's statements about the cocaine, and the fact that Jim smoked pot.

Some questions were answered, while others were not. There were still mental health issues prevalent in the months prior to my husband's death, but nothing that could explain his Dr. Jekyll, Mr. Hyde disposition.

* * * * * * *

Later that summer, my mother and I eventually moved into a nice flat in Lansingburgh. The memories were unbearable in Troy, and my mother wanted to be closer to High Gate Manor, for work.

Slowly, I began to get back into as normal of a routine as could be expected. Len and Sarah remained a big part of our lives, but due to the change of my work schedule, Jimmy and I were not seeing Sarah as often.

Jimmy was thriving and had started walking. He was also talking a mile a minute. As his first birthday approached, I could not help but think how proud his father would have been of him. I was also faced with having to plan a bittersweet celebration.

Every night at bedtime, I would lie quietly in my room and pray for Jim, telling him how much I loved him, thanking him for the wonderful memories we had made, and most importantly, for our beautiful little boy. Included in my prayers, I also wanted him to know that I had forgiven him; that I knew he was not himself, for a number of reasons.

I remember that I would fall asleep with tears streaming down my cheeks, soaking my pillow, wondering how life would have been had we not moved to Watervliet. I also knew that regardless, there was nothing that could be done to change what happened.

Most importantly, I would pray, and ask God to forgive Jim for committing suicide. I felt that since he had miraculously spared our lives that it was one of the greatest gifts that we could have been blessed with.

Through death, there was life that came in the precise moment that my mother connected with him, long enough to make him aware that he loved us. Yes, he had been fighting many demons, but in those split seconds born out of love, Good, momentarily triumphed over Evil.

Long ago, my grandmother taught me the significance of allowing spirits to appear on their own, unforced. She also encouraged prayer and meditation resting upon a foundation of positive thought, as the best approach to receive spirit messages. Always following her advice, I had found her guiding principles, to be true.

As it were, within a very short period of time, Jim would come through in dream, not just once, but twice. Each contact he presented would carry two very different messages. The first dream remains to be the most beautiful in meaning that I have ever had.

Standing alone on a mountaintop, I could see an amazing morning sky. The glorious hues of the sunrise were brilliant and breathtaking. Pink and orange streaks against a sapphire sky, the warm and glistening rays of sunlight filtered down on me, as I stood on the peak.

I remember looking around in wonderment of the view. I

did not see what was below me, but I could see the horizon and the sky. Words cannot do justice to what I saw, or how I felt.

The sunshine began to encompass the mountaintop: I was in awe of its beauty. Feeling someone take my hand, I looked to my side to find Jim standing next to me, smiling. I remember beginning to cry in my dream; he was perfect. He was happy.

Taking my other hand, we soon faced one another. He told me that he was thankful that I forgave him, and that he was sorry; he never wanted to hurt me. He told me how much he loved Jimmy and I, and asked me not to cry.

Telling me that he would always watch over us and protect us, he told me that it was time for him *to go*. With teardrops rolling down my face, I asked him if it was just a dream, to which he replied, "No," and embraced me.

As he held me, I noticed the sky began to open, as the sun's light became brighter, and brighter. Kissing me on my forehead, he let go of my hands and looked up towards the sky, and then faded into the most magnificent and pure, white light. With tears falling from my eyes, I knew that he had crossed.

Waking up, my face moist from the tears of slumber, I noted the date: August 8th, 1989. It was 40 days after his death.

Although it was difficult seeing him leave in the dream, I found a sense of comfort, knowing that he was at peace. I remember thinking that the dream was *heavenly*.

When later discussing the dream with my mother, she too, believed that if Jim had been possessed, it was entirely possible that with prayer and understanding, he would be forgiven and in turn, would be able to cross. Although I had found hope through the dream, I still continued to pray for him.

The second dream in which Jim appeared, was a stark contrast to the first; it scared the daylights out of me. It began with the ringing sound of a telephone; however, I could not find the phone to answer it. Stumbling through a very foggy and benign room, I finally saw the phone and picked it up.

The line was riddled with static and interference, and I remember that I could barely hear the voice on the other end. It was urging me to move closer to a partitioned wall that was

OPPRESSION & POSSESSION

veiled by a thick, gray mist.

Moving closer to the partition, the static began to clear; I could hear Jim's voice. He then asked me to watch the partition, as he appeared, wearing a white gauze garment. He looked very serious, and told me not to be afraid.

He then advised me that Jerry was going to kill himself and that I needed to warn our friends. This frightened me to the point that I remember trying to force myself awake. He asked me to hold onto the phone, as he professed his love and then faded away. I stood at the partition crying, when a single gunshot rang out. I then woke with my heart pounding. It was August 18th, 1989.

I was terrified. I had to take Jim's warning seriously – he insisted I do – but who was going to believe me? I knew my mother, grandmother, Karen and Carol would, but what about everyone else? I did not want to create an issue, but I also could not ignore Jim's request.

That morning, my mother suggested that I call Jerry to see how he was doing. Fair enough, but I did not want to say anything that would trigger Jerry's mind into some type of suggestive behavior. A fine line to walk, I had to at least try to make contact with him.

Taking place during the same time period, my mother had finally decided that it was time for her to quit smoking. She felt more so compelled, due to coming so close to being killed a couple of months prior. Having lost count at the number of previous attempts made to kick the habit, she was determined to give it one more try. She had used gums, patches, and even had quit cold turkey, yet nothing would work for more than a week or two.

This time was different though, she felt quite confident that she would be successful, as a coworker had given her the name of a reputable Hypnotist in Albany. From my standpoint, anything was worth a try, and I was going to support her, even with a round or two of hypnosis.

So, within a day or so of being given the information, my mother made an appointment to see Ann Fisher, Ph.D. She was motivated, and I was happy that she was trying to improve her health.

12

The Fall

Following Jim's death, Jerry would call every so often and ask if there was anything that Jimmy, or I needed. Always happy to hear from him, I would thank him, but never wanted to impose.

Overall, he did seem to have handled things as good as could be expected, but I did notice that with time, he called less frequently, and appeared to become more reticent. It was not until I made that call to feel things out, when an eerie conversation took place.

Initially speaking with a friend about Jimmy's upcoming birthday party, I asked how Jerry was doing. Noting some hesitation, the individual mentioned that Jerry had been going to the cemetery to visit Jim's grave, and had been known to drink a beer or two, at his gravesite. Somewhat normal, given Jim was his lifelong best friend, I remembering feeling slightly uncomfortable with the remark, especially when she had disclosed that Jerry had also visited 207 several times immediately following Jim's death, gaining access to the vacant apartment. Until then, I had only known of the time he and

143

Len had gone to clean out, and retrieve the items from the flat.

Taking a risk, I then told the friend about the warning that Jim had given me through my dream; she actually laughed, and stated Jerry would never do anything to hurt him self. She did admit that he had experienced a spell of depression after Jim's death, stating that it "wasn't a big deal." I specifically remember her stating that he would "snap out of it," too. I recall asking my friend to keep our conversation on the "Q-T," and recommended she keep her eyes and ears open relative to any more negative, or unusual behaviors.

Not happy to hear that Jerry had become depressed, I remember being a little miffed by my friend's flippant attitude, especially acknowledging that he was not himself. I also felt that it was not a good time to explain my abilities relative to spirit messages. I had accomplished what I was asked to do, and could only pray that Jerry would not take his life. The entire situation was out of my hands.

Come the day of Jimmy's birthday party, Jerry had decided to show up *after* the party, rather than during it. My mother and I talked to him as he sat and played with Jimmy, but we both noticed that his behavior was a bit off. I noticed almost the same type of disconnect that Jim had once exhibited. My senses were indicating that something was going on with him; he also seemed to have a muddy aura.

On Halloween, I took Jimmy to see my mother at work to cheer the patients. Dressed as a little pumpkin, my son's bubbly personality was a welcome surprise. Come late afternoon, we headed back to our apartment, where Jimmy was excited that he was going to hand out candy at the door.

Back then, Lansingburgh was a great family-oriented community, brimming with many children, most of whom had taken to the streets for some good, old-fashioned trick-or-treating. After a few rings of the doorbell, Jimmy had the routine down: He would run to the window to see who was standing outside, grab the small candy dish and carefully take the goodies to the door, wobbling all the way. What a thrill it was for him!

The flow of little candy collectors waned, with a handful of stragglers sporadically coming to the door in quest of last-minute fulfillment of a sugar quota. I remember that it was close to 8:30PM, when a special group of visitors presented themselves at our door: Jerry's girlfriend and her children.

Pleasantly surprised, I spoke with them as Jimmy handed out the candy, totally engrossed in one of the children's 'Alf' costumes. Just as they left the steps, I remember thinking that it was unusual that Jerry had not come with them. That was when his girlfriend made a remark that spooked me.

"Aren't you going to wave to Jerry?" she asked.

"Where the heck is he?" I responded. I did not see him anywhere.

"He's right over there – standing across the street," she answered, her tone in question of my inability to see him. "You can't see him waving?" she laughed.

"No, I can't, but I'll wave anyway! Hi, Jerry!" I yelled into the black, night air. "Jimmy, wave to Jerry!" I added, lifting my son into my arms.

"Hi, Jill and Jimmy. Happy Halloween," he responded, rather faintly. It was as though he was a million miles away.

Even now, I can recall the very bothersome feeling that I had. I couldn't even see an outline of him. His voice was also different; it lacked strength. More disturbing was the fact that I could not understand why he did not come over to say hello, choosing to stand across the street in the dark, as if he was intentionally avoiding us.

Speaking with my mother later that evening, I described what had happened, and that Jerry did not come to the door. I remember my mother remarking that it may have gotten too difficult for him to see us, adding that perhaps his depression was more serious than the friend had thought. Whether she was right or not, I did not like what I was sensing; it was all too familiar.

I will never, ever forget the call that I received from Sarah on November 2nd, 1989. Answering the telephone, I could tell right away that something was wrong. From the onset of the conversation she had asked if my mother was home with me, to which I replied, "Yes." She then asked me to sit down.

"What's wrong?" I asked.

"Jerry's dead!" she blurted out, fighting back tears.

I was stunned, shocked – horrified. I remember repeating, "What happened? What happened?"

Hearing the distress in my voice, my mother rushed to my side, as Sarah described what few details she had: Jerry had committed suicide in his apartment the night prior, after locking himself in the bedroom. His girlfriend along with some of her family, were present, but unharmed at the time.

I felt as though the wind had been knocked out of me. Our conversation ended rather quickly, as Sarah and I were both too upset to talk. My mother was speechless.

After trying to get in touch with some other friends to better understand what had happened, I eventually made the decision to call Jerry's girlfriend and express my condolences. With good cause to be upset, she managed to tell me that Jerry had indeed, been plummeting into a very deep depression. I could never completely confirm the following information, but several mutual friends later told me what led up to Jerry's suicide.

Jerry had been spending a great deal of time visiting the flat at 207 until he could no longer access it, often sitting in the dark and empty apartment for hours at a time. He was also going to Jim's graveside for extended periods, drinking beer and talking to him.

Apparently, at some point in the early fall Jerry had started talking to *himself*. I had been told that he would isolate himself in the bathroom, or bedroom, and talk to Jim as though he was present in the room. As more time passed, his actions became more peculiar. Although several people had corroborated this information, it was unclear what the details were on the night he committed suicide.

Given the time he spent at 207, as well as his trips to Jim's gravesite and the change in his mannerisms, I could not help but think that the energy at the flat had intensified, and possibly contributed to his depression. I was also convinced it had something to do with his suicide. This was now a third death of a male, due to a self-inflicted gunshot wound.

My last memory of Jerry was beyond strange, considering what happened on Halloween. To know that he killed himself one night later, was like throwing salt into an open wound.

I knew that I had passed along Jim's message, and did exactly what he had asked, but nobody took me seriously. It just hurt something fierce to know that considering these points, Jerry had taken his life, too.

The entire ordeal weakened me. In turn, I could not find the strength to attend Jerry's funeral; it was far too painful. Choosing to send a blanket of roses and greens to drape over his casket, I summed up my feelings as best as I could: We love you, and will miss you. God bless, Jill and Jimmy.

* * * * * * *

A minor distraction to what had transpired in early November, my mother had grown quite excited about seeing Ann Fisher, with hopes of putting an end to over thirty years of heavy smoking. Never having known of anyone to achieve success by means of hypnosis, it was a fascinating idea. Having been given recommendations to Ann by fellow nurses, my mother was cautiously optimistic, and eager to get started.

At the last minute, I decided to bring Jimmy with us, rather than find a sitter. The weather remained pleasant enough to take him for a walk, had he become fidgety.

Discussing the aspect of hypnosis, and how it worked relative to addictions, I remember reminding my mother that willpower was the key; she had to make up her mind to do it. A nurse with an excellent track record and education, she knew that to be the truth, but her lack of willpower when it involved smoking, had continue to remain her greatest nemesis.

Situated in Washing Park, Albany, I remember being challenged to find a parking space close to Ann's office. I also remember having a twinge in my stomach – not nausea – but a strange feeling, as the three of us walked along Willett Street.

Bright and pleasant, her office was filled with usual reading material, and was comparable to any other private office. After my mother had checked-in, Ann called her back to begin the session, as I sat and read to Jimmy.

The entire time that I remained in the waiting area, even though I had been reading to Jimmy, I remember having the sensation that something profound was floating around in the Universe. Patiently, I held my breath, hoping and praying that Ann would be successful in helping my stubborn mother.

"She can't hypnotize me," my mother remarked, walking through the door with a scowl, a short while later. "I'm too obstinate. I'm never going to be able to quit," she grumbled.

Seeing her disappointment, Ann replied, "You're just a strong-willed individual. These things happen."

I myself, was disappointed, let alone my poor mother. It seemed that no matter what she tried to do, her willpower – or lack thereof – always got the best of her. Having been told of Ann's high success rate, I knew that my mother was just one tough cookie.

Thinking that we were through, my mother then exclaimed that Ann was a Psychic, too. I felt that twinge in my stomach again. "Oh, really?" I replied.

I recall my mother stating that although Ann could not hypnotize her, she would give my mother a reading. My mother thought that would be interesting given the events of the last year, and agreed to it. Asking if I would like one to follow, I remember thinking that it wouldn't be a bad idea at all, and consented to the participation.

There I was: One minute waiting for my mother to finish a hypnosis session, and the next, waiting to have an impromptu psychic reading. Could the day have taken any stranger of a turn?

Approximately sixty minutes later, my mother trotted back to the waiting room, looking as though she had seen a ghost. Taking Jimmy in her lap, she briefly remarked how accurate Ann had been, and told me that it was my turn.

A very homey space, Ann's office had a modest desk with chairs, and a comfortable looking sofa set against the far wall. Dimly lit, I considered that the room had been left that way to facilitate a comfortable state for hypnosis. I also remember that as I looked away from the couch, I experienced a very strong shift in energy, but not negative in nature. I felt as though Jim had walked through the door. My heart quickened, as I had not experienced that after his passing.

Welcoming me into her office, Ann was extremely polite and warm. Noticing several educational plaques on the wall, I was able to see how well educated she was. Also, based upon the number, and variety of books scattered about, she appeared to be very well read on several topics.

"Your husband is here – over by the couch. He is very sorry for what he did – for what he put you through," she stated, as my heart began to pound. It *was* him!

"You are very lucky. Even though he tried to kill you, he protected you. He was possessed," she added as I sat shaking in my chair.

"There were supposed to be two other deaths that night; you and your son, but your mother brought him back. He saved you both," she continued.

I began to weep, nodding to the affirmative, plucking tissues from a box. She then paused for a moment and flinched, as if she had sensed something.

"I hear another gunshot. Someone else died? A brother – no wait – a friend, his best friend. He was also affected by the same thing that possessed your husband," she stated in a slightly excited tone. "Where is this place? I need to know, if you can tell me," she added. The air in the room grew very warm.

Dear Lord in Heaven, I remember thinking, how could this be? How did she know this information? Had my mother said something to her?

Confirming what she had said, I listened as she stated that the location of my husband's death was a key to what had happened. I also waited for her to mention the energies that

I had sensed, or the other individual who had committed suicide in 207, years prior to Jim's death.

She told me that Jimmy and I were going to be just fine and paused again. Ann then stated something that I knew she would definitely not have any knowledge of: She knew that Jim had come to me through my dreams and had warned me about Jerry's death. Pausing again, she then added that she felt I had some powerful abilities myself, and needed to pay attention to them, rather than ignore them.

Asking my birthday, she quickly conducted jotted down some numbers, stating that I had a very keen sense of abilities to communicate with the deceased, and was also highly clairvoyant. She also mentioned my past lives, and then went on to describe some of my personality traits, highlighting both strengths and weaknesses.

Just before our session concluded, Ann asked me to do some homework. She felt a strong need to identify whatever her inkling was relative to 207, only making reference to it as being "very dangerous." Wanting to 'read' the energy, she asked me to bring photographs to my future appointment. I was then issued a stern warning:

I was to never step foot in that house, or on that property, ever again. She also told me that the same applied to my son. Considering that he was a baby, she implored that at some point when he was older, he would need to be advised of that, as well. Her cautionary statement was unnerving.

Concerned that I had returned to the house to get items the prior July, she said that I would not have a problem, so long as I had not taken anything with me, or returned. Ironically, and as I explained to her, I had left in a hurry, without taking one single item.

Questioning if it was safe for me and Jimmy to drive along 19th Streets and 2nd Avenue by car, she approved; however, stated that I should not walk on the property, or go in to the house. No problem with that – I had no intention to do either.

Assuring Ann that I would gather some photographs of the house and schedule a reading, I left the room. I recall how remarkably cooler it was after opening the office door. Our spontaneous session had become rather intense. I also remember looking over my shoulder, towards the area that Ann had said Jim stood, and whispering a sullen, "Goodbye, Jim. I love you." I sensed he had left.

Jimmy had behaved like a little angel throughout the unscheduled meetings. Thanking Ann for giving us the opportunity, my mother made a joke about her failure to be hypnotized, and we left. What an afternoon!

Curious was an understatement. Before I began to disclose my amazing session with Ann, I had to make sure that my mother had not accidentally, or intentionally given Ann any information about Jim.

"Did you tell her anything about Jim, or me?" I asked.

"No, I didn't. Why?" she replied. My mother also stated that that Ann was dead-on, about details of her own past. She also knew that my mother had saved our lives.

I told her everything that took place in our session, and when mentioning that Ann had stated her belief that Jim and Jerry were possessed, remember she quickly blessed herself. As insane as it sounded, things were certainly pointing in that direction.

With the Christmas holiday approaching, I decided to wait until after New Year's, to go back to Ann. Between family events, and trying to coordinate Jimmy's visitation with my in-laws, I felt it was best to take some time and let things calm down. I also had to go through some of my photographs for Ann, which included collecting any that showed our tree in the very spot Jim had died, and where the spirit of that man had first appeared. This would be the first Christmas after Jim's death and I knew it was going to be very difficult.

* * * * * * *

Scheduling a large brunch for Christmas morning, I had invited Jim's entire family. My maternal grandmother was also visiting for the holidays, and as challenging as it would be, the thought of having everyone together for Jimmy, was somewhat comforting.

With plans confirmed on Christmas Eve, pre-brunch preparation had taken place in the kitchen, as my grandmother, an avid Cook, helped to make muffins and cookies. Our goal was to minimize time spent cooking on Christmas morning, so that the three of us could enjoy the day, and later go out to dinner in the evening.

Ten o'clock Christmas morning came with no sign of Jim's family. Eleven o'clock, and we still had not heard from them. It was close to twelve o'clock when I had finally received a call, stating that they were late in getting a ride and would be there as soon as they could. So much for brunch, I thought: It looked more like lunch.

It was not until close to two o'clock when they all arrived. I remember that my mother and grandmother were very upset, as my in-laws knew that we had dinner plans. Although there was obvious tension relative to a slightly rushed lunch, they were able to spend some time with Jimmy, and that was what mattered most.

13

Nun Sense

Len and Sarah had invited Jimmy and I, over for their 1990 New Year's Eve celebration. It was so nice to know that considering all of the turmoil, they had remained such close friends.

Among good people, and with my son by my side, we rang in the New Year together. Some of us cried, knowing what a heart-breaking year that it had been.

With the energy of 207 stalking the neighborhood, and located right next door, I remember feeling apprehensive about being there. Still, Ann had said not to walk on the property, or in the house. We were safe so long as we stayed within the confines of Len and Sarah's yard, but not a single foot would be placed on the property that I had deemed "The Gateway to Hell."

If my memory serves me correctly, it was a couple of weeks after the new-year when I had scheduled my appointment with Ann Fisher. Gathering photos of the room that had been taken on Christmas of 1988, I also wanted to see if she could pick up on the window, which had been the focus of Chris' dreams, as well as the location of the silhouettes. I wanted to know what she thought about the evil entities that had taken up home in the flat.

Ann's professional, yet sincere disposition had once more made me feel comfortable, which was a blessing given the context of the visit. Carefully placing the photos on her desk, she examined them in silence. When finished, she held out one particular photo, which showed the side of the living room with the fireplace, and pointed to the right hand corner.

"That's where your husband died," she confidently stated.

My heart skipped a beat or two, as I acknowledged that she was correct. She then held up the photo of Jim sitting on the couch. To his left, was the controversial window, which had been the subject of quite a bit of the paranormal activity. Little doubt remained; something very sinister was attached to that area of the house.

With that very photograph, Ann stated that another male had committed suicide in the room, and that he too, had been possessed. All that I could offer for reference was that the man had lived in the flat at some point during the 1960's, or 1970's.

Ann then went on to state that she felt there was spirit energy of another male, and that of a nun. She said that both were somehow connected by a *church,* or regarding churches, in general. She went on to state that demonic energy existed in the house and in our flat in particular, and had been present for many, many years. Emphasizing danger, I remember that I began to feel quite overwhelmed. I also remembered what my grandmother had once said about a church connection!

Extremely concerned, Ann had asked me for the name and telephone number of my former Landlord. She also wanted the address to the flat. She said that she felt strongly that the property would need an exorcism, and was going to make some phone calls to see if she could relay the importance of her reading, to him. She also mentioned that she would have liked to conduct a séance at the flat, on the next full moon: That made my skin crawl. I also remember hoping that my former Landlord, who had known of the history, would be willing to let her help. She made it very clear that peoples' lives could be in danger, due to the malevolent energy that had rooted itself in the house.

After giving her the information, Ann asked me if I had known whether a nun had ever lived in the flat: That, I could not confirm. She explained that she knew that the male energy was dangerous, but was not as wicked as the nun. She stated that the nun was *exceptionally evil*. Elaborating, she stated that the spirits of these individuals had possessed the former resident, Jim and even Jerry, due to their weakened states. Manifesting itself through the man and the nun, she added that the energy was demonic, and had been "running the house" for decades.

She then asked if there was a church nearby, by which I replied that St. Patrick's Cathedral, was just to the west of 207. Raising her brow, I could see that her curiosity had deepened.

With the possibility of a nun being factored into the paranormal activity, I immediately told her about the only identifiable energy that I could discern while we had lived there. Explaining that it was that of an older male, dressed in black with piercing eyes, he had authoritarian traits, and a threatening presence. I also explained that the spirit seemed to feed-off of the larger, more violent energy. Ann felt that there was definitely a connection, but said that she really needed to get into the house to better 'read' it. She also made a comment that has stuck in my mind.

"That house really should be torn down. The same thing is going to continue to happen to the Tenants unless it is exorcised. Even then, it may still need to be torn down. The energy of the nun is violent, and full of hate. She wanted you dead -- you *and* your son." Those were pretty powerful words, and I became queasy to hear her speak so assuredly.

We then discussed my abilities in relationship to having lived in a 'haunted house.' She asked me to describe, in as great of detail as possible, the way the house made me feel, in addition to the frightening events that took place.

Ann then took the time to describe the differences between the symptoms of demonic oppression and demonic possession.

Summarizing demonic oppression, traits such as unusual anxiety and fear, lack of self-control and outbursts of aggression, hatred and even violence, manifest in a susceptible host. I believe this to be Jim's case early on, shortly after moving into the flat.

She then continued to explain symptoms of a demonic possession, which include mania, intense aggression, unnatural facial expressions, obsession with pornography, violent and reckless behaviors, distancing from God for fear of being cast-out, split personality, depression, despondent behavior, murder and suicide. All by which were existent in, and dominant of Jim's behavior, for the last six months of his life.

Given her theory on what may have transpired in the flat, I had a better understanding as to why I was unable to identify the energies. What she described as a combination of my lack of experience in dealing with negative, or evil energies, in addition to the energy disguising it self and feeding off of Jim, as well as my ability to 'block' it, concealed its true nature. She also said that it was a very good thing that I prayed for protection, and had blessed the house myself, even if I did not think it had worked.

Ann also made another startling connection. Having merely suggested that Father conduct a house blessing, in conjunction to Jim's response to my requests, as well as his putting a stop to my attempt to contact Father, she felt was the demonic energy creating conflict. The energy had oppressed and possessed Jim, and was afraid of being forced out; it was using Jim as a vehicle to do its work. Bringing to light the fact that we had experienced a horrid odor just days before Jimmy's baptism, and Jim's behavior towards my grandmother's photograph of the Pope, and strangely hiding our crucifix: It all made frightening sense. It was at this point in time, that three people had independently stated their belief that my husband had been possessed: My grandmother, our priest and Ann.

Further advising me, she stated that it was important for me to be strong and never to use my abilities for anything negative, of which I agreed and told her I would not do. I remember concluding the session and being thankful that after all of this time, even though it was too late as far as Jim and Jerry were concerned, that a last-minute change of plans, and my mother's concrete stubbornness, had put me in touch with Ann.

I remember feeling relieved that she had helped make sense out of all of the unusual activity and behaviors that were experienced in connection with 207. I felt so blessed that she was also able to provide insight and help, relative to my own abilities.

Mentioning my meeting to Carol and my mother, as well as my grandmother, we were all in agreement that tearing down the house would probably be the best thing to do, given its history. It was no longer coincidence that seemed to tie many events together. Receiving quite an eye-opening education as to the paranormal, and demonic oppression and possession, I prayed that through all of the pain and sorrow, I would be better prepared to help others in the future. I did not want to see anyone else suffer as all of us had, including Jim and Jerry.

As spring of 1990 approached, I had wondered whether or not Ann had been able to get in touch with my former Landlord, but prayed that the saga of 207 would come to a close without anyone else being harmed. I would cringe and look away, every time I had to pass that house, while driving to, and from, Troy. It was a hellish reminder of more than twelve months of trauma and excruciating emotional, and physical pain.

One day, however, I had noticed what appeared to be new Tenants living in the flat. They were sitting on the steps in front of 207 on a warm, late June day, very close to the anniversary of Jim's death.

Looking only long enough to see they were talking to a few others who had gathered around, I could not help but wonder if they were experiencing anything unusual. I sensed that *something* was occurring, but it was not for me to be concerned about.

* * * * * * *

Wanting to reconnect with Ann one more time, I scheduled another appointment. I had many questions since our last meeting. Of particular interest, I wanted to know if she had been able to convince my former Landlord, to let her conduct a séance and, or, exorcism.

Leaving Jimmy in the care of my mother, I drove to Albany to see Ann. She immediately stated that she had suggested the house be torn down, but offered few details. She seemed a bit anxious about the topic, almost slightly stressed. She did, however, want to make sure that I had taken her warning seriously, during our last visit. After assuring her that I had, she then said that there was nothing more that could be done, other than to demolish the property. She also stated that it would not be wise to rebuild on the property. Expressing concern for the new Tenants, she restated that it was extremely dangerous for *anyone* to live there.

For the remainder of our session, we discussed what was happening in my life. We also conversed about her involvement in helping various police agencies solve some crimes, including serial killer Lemuel Smith's, murder spree. Smith held Albany by the clench of his homicidal fist, as he conducted a reign of terror throughout the city in the mid-to-late '70's. Ann would later be featured on the television show "Psychic Detectives," for her involvement in helping to crack the case.

From the few meetings that I had shared with her, and upon learning of the scope of her work in relationship to helping solve crimes, I could not help but think what a remarkable, intelligent woman she was. She had definitely made a positive impact on my life, and was using her abilities to help the community with her gifts; something that I would later strive to do.

Ann and I had a rather profound conversation on how great good can be attained with "gifts" by helping others. Both my mother and grandmother had always said that God brings people into your life for a reason, and Ann walked into mine at a time where she was definitely needed the most.

Thanking her for taking me under her wing, so to speak, we

parted ways, as I promised her that I would follow by example, and help others. I also reassured her that I would at some point tell my son about her words of warning. That would be the last time that I would see Ann, until June of 2005, as I had moved out of the Albany area.

With each passing day, I reflected upon life. I was truly blessed that Jimmy and I were saved by my mother's courage; she was without one single doubt, my Heroine. Always modest, she would often state that she only did what any other mother would do. To her, saving our lives was not an option, nor something that needed time to consider; it was something that needed to be done.

Each and every one of those random, hell-raising, unbelievable, inexplicable events shaped one of the darkest moments of time in my life. Ironically, they also helped to cultivate my sense of spirituality, and in turn, provided me strength; a strength that I never knew I had, until my world fell apart on that horrifying June night.

14

Endings & Beginnings

The series of tragic events that took place in just over a year's time, caused great personal agony, but also made me realize the importance of spirituality. Looking back to the days following my husband's death, I recall an experience that would define that sentiment, and it all began with a massive sinus infection – believe it, or not.

The intense headache and pressure was one of the most physically painful that I have ever had. After undergoing an emergency C.T. and M.R.I., it was determined that I was suffering from "Cavernous Sinus Thrombosis," a very dangerous infection that required hospitalization for a handful of days, and a lengthy course of antibiotics.

During the stay, due to the recent loss of my husband, my E.N.T. doctor thought it was a good idea to have me speak with a Psychologist to make sure that I would be able to pull through the crisis physically, as well as emotionally.

I recall the physician quietly entering my room, and pulling up a chair to speak with me. One of his first comments was directed at how horribly swollen my eyes and cheekbones had become.

After our initial introduction, he urged me to place the cold compresses back over my head, informing me that we would talk about my husband's death, and all of the emotions it encompassed. I was beyond emotionally exhausted.

Recounting the events that transpired was difficult, but I remember that it actually felt very good to speak with someone removed from the drama. Stoic in nature, he sat and listened as I told him about the moments that I thought my son and I were going to be killed.

In detail, I described how I felt when my mother had become aware that Jim was holding the shotgun to my son and I. I also expressed how after several minutes of negotiating, my mother had been able to reach Jim, and persuade him to put the gun down just long enough to leave.

I remember that the doctor seemed very interested in my description of Jim's face, as I compared it to that of a monster, and how it changed the very moment my mother was able to reason with him. I compared his actions to the similarity of being shocked back into reality, as it appeared that he had no idea what he was doing with the gun in hand, when that brief moment occurred.

The doctor also asked me how *I* felt. I told him that I was devastated, but knew that my husband was not well. The fact that he had left without killing us was a miracle, and the fact that my mother acted in the way she had, was astonishing. I also expressed that I was sure that we would not be alive had it not been her quick thinking and selfless love. Through the raging actions of a man gone mad, we were somehow spared: I felt incredibly thankful, and blessed.

The Psychologist then told me that he felt that I was remarkably strong, even though I had faced some very dramatic and unfortunate circumstances. He said that my willingness to share the events and my feelings was a very therapeutic means of dealing with the tragedy. He also told me never to stop doing that. Additionally, he suggested that I could one day use my experiences to help others, who may endure a similar crisis.

He then remarked, "Jill, you've been through more than most people will have to endure in an entire lifetime, and you're only twenty-four-years-old. You're a strong woman, and you are going to do well." He then paused, and told me that my attitude was commendable, wished me to feeling better, and left the room.

Having always been told that I am a strong person, I could not help but wonder why there would be an option for me *not* to be okay. As far as I was concerned, there was no other choice.

The fact that Jim spared our son's life, as well as my mother and mine, was one of the biggest blessings that I could ever ask for. I was able to grieve for Jim, yet there was no time to feel sorry for myself; I had to move forward through the anguish. Giving up was *never* an option.

While recovering from the infection, I found that it was my spirituality, not so much religious faith that I relied upon, to get me through the sorrow. I knew that no matter what, *I* was personally responsible for maintaining a *realistic* sense of hope and optimism, even when my world seemed to have instantly crumbled away.

This also helped me better understand how others, who may not be able to deal with such tragedy, were in need of spiritual strengthening. Through such deep sorrow, I had discovered that I wanted to help others recognize, that even in their darkest moments, there is hope – and that hope is found through reliance on one's Spiritual Self.

* * * * * * *

I whole-heartedly believe that if it were not for the inner strength that I maintained during those events, even at the early onset just after moving into 207 19th Street, I would not have made it out alive. I have developed the following rationale, relative to what transpired back then.

I think that my abilities as a Medium and Clairvoyant, actually helped keep me balanced. I do think that my aptitude for 'blocking' out the negative energy, actually facilitated my survival in the flat.

'Blocking' is something that I had learned to do whenever I picked up on uncomfortable energies. Still somewhat inexperienced at the time, I had fortunately developed enough of my abilities to be able to do so both automatically, as well as intentionally.

Unfamiliar with demonic energy, I had the capability to sense something dark – but had no idea what it *was*. At a loss as to how to best handle the situation, I had to rely on instinct, as well as my grandmother for most guidance.

With hindsight, I can see how my grandmother was reluctant to explain exactly what she had felt, and helped shield us as best as she could, through prayer. I also believe that prayer was a major means to deflect the evil, and ultimately increased my chances of survival, as well.

Prayer is of notable interest given the fact that quite a bit of contact with the negative energy came through during sleep, in the form of dreams. Not only occurring in *my* dream state, Chris and Jim had experiences, too.

Every night that I slept in that apartment, I made sure to pray and ask for protection, all the while 'blocking' as much as I could from a psychic standpoint. Someone that may not have done so, in addition to being under the influence of drugs and, or alcohol, would have made themselves more vulnerable to the invasion of demonic forces, creating greater risk for oppression and, or possession.

This is a very significant parallel to Jim. After moving in to 207 19th Street, his drinking and binging soared. Prior to the move, he seemed to be able to control himself, inclusive of his drinking. Also factoring into the equation is his use of drugs, such as marijuana and apparently cocaine. It was bad enough to drink, let alone partake in street drugs, in that type of setting. Further considering Jim's damaged psyche from enduring great suffering throughout his childhood, the move to 207 created the perfect storm for the demonic energy to thrive, and destroy all who wandered into its unholy realm.

Having 'blocked' what I was able to, there still lingered a very uneasy feeling that literally grew with every passing day. The oppression and possession theory made startling sense, looking back to those specific incidents. Understanding that it is a matter of speculation supported by factual events and changes in my husband's behavior that took place *after* the move, it is one that is strongly considered.

In agreement that Jim was in a world of trouble in the legal sense, was dealing with at least alcohol abuse problems, had disclosed some very agonizing trauma, and was about to go through a divorce, it is only natural to draw reference to suicidal tendencies in a person with a fragile state of mind. I do, however, have to say that I am certain the atmosphere of 207 compounded those matters, negatively impacting his psyche, and chewing-away at his spirituality. The fact remains that his behavior went haywire, after moving in to the house.

In reference to our personal relationship: I loved my husband with all of my heart and soul. Throughout our three years together, we remained very close; he meant the world to me. I was truly torn to see him go through what he did, and more so, to know that he felt he had no other choice than to end his life.

Until we took residence in that house, he had never been out of control emotionally, mentally, or physically to the point of which he was in the months prior to his death. On the day of his suicide, he was not the same man that I married, but if for sake of the last memory that I have of him, I saw something of his former self fight those demons, in the split seconds he chose to leave without taking anyone else's lives: I knew that he loved me.

By examining the information, it is reasonable to correlate what happened, to an oppression, and possession. Perhaps the most significant indications of this theory have to do with the other changes that had taken place during that year.

My husband never had a problem going to church for services, and Father had been an integral part of his life since he was a child. For Jim to make such a fast about-face, without justification or provocation, indicates that the energies in the flat eyed him as an easy target, and attacked him.

To start, just prior to my son's baptism, we had experienced the mystery odor. Come the day of the ceremony, Jim was already exhibiting some irritation, which was unusual for him in that type of setting.

Other indicators were an increasing hostility and violent attitude towards the house blessing, my grandmother's photograph of the Pope, along with his removal of our crucifix over our bed, and his reaction to my reading the Bible when I was so frightened. The house was trying to feed off of our energy, especially Jim's, positioning itself to take control of at least one of us. The energies were afraid of God.

From another perspective relative to traits, Jim's wild personality changes were truly strange. His mannerisms had even changed, from the look in his eyes, to his speech pattern and vocabulary. It was as if he was a different person at times. When angered, his green eyes turned black; a wicked fiend taking control of his body, mind and soul, in short bursts.

Come June 28th, 1989, there was undoubtedly premeditated intent to take our lives, but ironically, the instantaneous flash of reality that came over him, connected with the 'old Jim' long enough for him to put the gun down. I believe that connection came from a place of love and goodness, which very briefly had triumphed over Evil. The demons may have tried to take over his mind, but there was still a part of his heart that my husband was able to grasp and fight with, which ultimately helped save the lives of my mother, son and I.

However, inexplicable, I knew that I had to be strong. I held on to my spirituality as a guiding force to combat the unseen enemy.

Praying for your life is an experience that I hope nobody will ever have to face, and given the amount of praying that I did, it is a sad reminder of Jim's inability to protect *him self.* Mentally, physically, emotionally and spiritually depleted, Jim was helpless. There was little anyone else could do to save him, albeit a possible exorcism, which had not even crossed a single mind. Since then, I have often wondered if Father would have been able to pick up on the energies had he conducted a blessing, and question if he may even have been able to save my husband's life.

* * * * * * *

There is something very real that exists in this world, which thrives on chaos, turmoil, destruction, and death: Its name is Evil. Regardless of manner, it creeps in and out of life, fearing what is good and righteous; fearing God. That is why one of the biggest ways to combat such forces, is by maintaining spiritual strength during attacks, and life crisis.

Evil energy can wear down anyone, and will most certainly prey on those weak in spirit. That is why in cases relative to oppression and possession, it is extremely important to reach out for help, and take the proper measures to protect yourself, whether by happenchance, or on a paranormal investigation.

Countless times, I have told both of my sons that no matter what path they take relative to faith and religion, it is personal spirituality that is the foundation and springboard for getting through life. When the going gets tough, there are two options: Giving up, or getting up. A strong sense of spirituality will help protect you, and give you the confidence and strength that is needed to surmount life's obstacles, including hatred, adversity, and all things negative.

Spirituality is something that grows with life experience. It teaches each and every one of us to be strong. Through wisdom that comes with age, it is enhanced and develops into a guiding force to see us through trials, and tribulations.

Spirituality is also very individualistic. It is created out of personal growth, based upon a unique blueprint and series of life events that shapes the Spiritual Self. Given this, each one of us arrives at different levels of spirituality, at different times.

The intrinsic value of spirituality remains a conscious decision. It is also a form of self-reliance; no matter what, you are going to have to make an effort to call on your Spiritual Self to stand strong. Nobody can do it for you; it comes from within.

Spirituality is also timeless. Never totally leaving the Self, it remains rooted in the soul even when one may question their path -- and it always lets you know it's there. The simple act of questioning your life is actually your Spiritual Self letting you know that you hold the key to find the answers; you hold the solution to your happiness, and life purpose. It also transcends time, after death in the physical sense.

Education, awareness, and a strong sense of spirituality are the weapons that will help win the fight against Evil. From the birth of the Universe, until its demise, the epic battle will surely rage, bringing forth great joy and inexplicable pain, to those who get caught in the crossfire.

If you take anything away from reading this book, I would ask that beginning today, each and every one of you become more aware of your own spirituality, and quest to nourish a stronger Spiritual Self. It does not take a special place or time, to make a needed start; it only takes a deep desire that speaks from within the heart, and soul.

EPILOGUE

Several years ago, after taking a trip back home to New York, I had noticed that 207 19th, as well as most of the block at the intersections of 19th Street and 2nd Avenue, had been torn down, inclusive of Len and Sarah's house. Considering that most of the block had been bulldozed for commercial development and revitalization of the area, I could not help but wonder what happened to the demonic energy that existed in the house.

Oddly situated, and perhaps the only reminder of the row of 19th and 20th Century homes which once had lined the block, sits a single house, a few lots west of the former 207. Of plain and unassuming construction, it lends no indication to the horror that had unfolded at its neighbor's, over the course of many years. The lot of 207, now a driveway and parking area for a drugstore, has become an ironic metaphor for the sick and murderous energies that plagued the original structure.

I remember picking up a very eerie vibe in July of 2006, and then again as I had passed by that location, in February of 2008. My abilities kicked into overdrive as I sensed a change in the energy, relative to the area: I did not like what I was 'reading,' and knew that I would have to investigate my suspicions when it came time to author this book.

Addressed at the beginning of this book, I had to give careful thought to my oldest son Jimmy, before I jumped in to tackle my hunch. It was not until just before my son had entered high school, when I, with the support of my two best friends and my mother, told my son that his father had committed suicide.

For years, I had told him that he had been drinking the night he died, but I *never* told him that he had been killed in a car accident. I also told Jimmy that his father had undergone a string of serious personal problems, close to the time of his death.

As advised by a coworker at the hospital as to how best handle the situation, I agreed that it was paramount, to let him bring up the subject, and ask questions on his own accord. I always answered him honestly, using his age and ability to process the information at various stages, as a guide. The older my son became, the more information that I would reveal, completely excluding anything to do with the paranormal.

There were three people *directly* involved in my life at the time of Jim's death: My mother, Carol and Karen. Anyone else was far removed from what transpired on a *daily* basis, with some remaining in the loop, but on the periphery. The three of us agreed that together, we would answer Jimmy's questions with truth, when it came time for him to know of the entire history.

When the opportunity presented itself, my son did considerably well, even mentioning that he had always had a feeling something "different" had happened to his father. He stated this because in the past, I did not say anything other than he had been drinking and had been in a lot of trouble.

Nonetheless, I, along with Carol, Karen and my mother, were able to let him how very much his father loved him, regardless of what had happened. It was not until several years later, that we discussed the other extenuating issues, relative to paranormal activity, in addition to the theories of oppression, and possession.

With both of my now adult sons bearing witness to my abilities, it did not come to much of a surprise to hear what transpired in the flat at 207. I had also wanted their opinions as to what they thought about the oppression and possession theories. Together, they agreed that it all seemed far too coincidental, and extremely peculiar.

Even they suggested that I publicly share my account. Informing them that the very idea had been discussed for years, amongst my closest friends and family members, it was with their blessings that I began to put forth the effort.

In addition to the premise of the book, I wanted to make certain that they were at a point in their lives whereas they could handle some of the potential backlash that may occur, upon the release of the book. I knew that the time had come to do so, as they both expressed that they were comfortable with the situation, and supportive of me.

Prompted by a psychic sense relative to my assessment of the change in energy around the property in Watervliet, in addition to the need to conduct some investigative journalism for sake of the book, I decided to make a long anticipated phone call to the store. It had been on my mind for years.

Slightly hesitant to reach out, I was aware that the recipients of my call would either think that I was two paddles short a canoe, or that they would assist me with my query. Either way, I knew that I had to put forth the effort.

A majority of my concern centers around employees and residents, located within direct vicinity of the old lot. Given what had taken place in the past, combined with the alteration in the atmosphere surrounding the store, I had to be sure that at the very least, they were free from paranormal activity. And so, with my youngest son sitting next to me, and the telephone on speaker mode, I apprehensively placed the call to the store that was built very close to 207's lot.

With my mind racing and my face flushed, I explained that I needed to obtain some information. After being placed on a brief hold, a different store employee picked up on the call.

I began by telling the individual that I am a Spiritual

Medium and Clairvoyant, whose been writing a book about events that transpired in the area during the late 1980's. Not wanting to waste their time, I then asked if the individual knew of any paranormal activity that may have been taking place in the store, or on its property.

In order to get an objective answer, I advised the employee that I would later explain the logic behind my odd questions. Additionally, I had asked if they were from the local area, or had knowledge of the property's history. The employee stated that they were not from the Watervliet area, nor had knowledge of any history. They did, however, state that they, as well as other associates, have witnessed some rather unusual paranormal activity in the store.

The individual then continued to detail the strange events, which had turned them from "a skeptic, into a believer." As I listened, they conveyed their experiences with unsettling disquietude.

Once the individual had finished explaining their personal encounters, they mentioned other employees who had also witnessed additional, disturbing events. This individual also mentioned that one associate in particular, Candace, had felt the store was haunted, and had been stating so for a considerable period of time. The employee also stated that collectively, they were stumped as to the cause for the activity.

The employee was quite a bit taken-back when I provided a shortened version of what had transpired in 207. They sounded relieved to know what they had witnessed, could possibly be explained. In their words they responded, "I knew that I wasn't going crazy."

Making the call during a holiday weekend afforded a small window of time for me to speak with Candace, whom had been expressing sentiments about the store's apparent haunt. My intention was to give her my contact information as to discuss the store's paranormal problems, after she had finished her shift, or while "off the clock." Speaking briefly, we exchanged information and agreed to talk later.

Before ending the phone call, I asked one last-minute

question to hold me over until we had an opportunity to speak: I inquired as to whether or not, a specific area of the store had seemed more prone to activity, than another. Candace immediately informed me that the left-hand side, second story of the store, was most active. This information bore great significance in the relationship 207, and its sordid past.

A million thoughts ran through my mind while waiting for her to return my call that night. Making a small list of specific questions, I had hoped to be able to identify what type of energies they were dealing with. Trying to remain objective, I kept reverting back to the feelings that had grown stronger over the last five years, or so. Something had changed in that environment, and I was becoming edgy giving consideration to the cause.

Approximately an hour later, the employee returned my call. Going into great detail about the history, she was amazed that some of the pieces to her own paranormal puzzle, had started to come together. As with the other employee, I noticed a sense of relief in her voice as I disclosed the actual history; it validated their collection of stories.

Coincidentally, with experience in Demonology and working as part of a paranormal investigative team, Candace began to draw reference between what I had revealed, and what was being experienced in the store by some of the employees. In agreement, it appears that the energies from 207 have possibly invaded the commercial property. When discussing the store's most recent activity, in comparison to even a few years prior, there seems to be an escalation in phenomenon.

One night, just after closing, a store associate had witnessed a disturbing image on one of the security cameras. It appeared as though a shadow figure of man, had darted between aisles, crouching low to the ground, seeking refuge in the next aisle. Within seconds after noticing the shadow figure on camera, the security lights illuminated the store, and the alarm sounded. There have been at least two occasions that have sent the Watervliet Police Department on break-in calls, but upon arrival, and after inspection, the store was found to be "secure and clear" of any person, mischief or animal trespass. The employee had stated that they were very shaken by the incident involving the shadow figure, and mentioned that it also puzzled the police. It was rendered as an inexplicable situation, or a "false alarm."

Another instance occurred when an employee began arranging newspapers for the morning opening of the store. Carrying bundled piles of the newspapers, they had returned to the staging area to find that one stack had been moved, although nobody else was around. The employee found this to be very unnerving.

Other associates have claimed to hear disembodied voices and sounds, inclusive of footsteps walking on the left side, second story of the store, and plastic stacking chairs being dragged around the aisles. Having occurred several times, nothing can be identified upon inspection of the area and review of surveillance camera footage. This has been noted by groups of employees working together. Candace has tried to debunk some of the issues, but has not been able to find reasonable cause. These accounts continue to remain a mystery.

Other unsolved mysteries involve the store's music system. With the controls being located upstairs, there have been times when the music becomes extremely loud, although no employee has physically turned it up. At other times, the music becomes distorted, as though there is an interference affecting the broadcast. From static, to humming, technicians working on the problem have not yet found any wiring issues, or other potential problems that could be contributing to the trouble.

The same occurs with the lighting on the left-hand side, second story. There are many times when the lights will turn on and off, although nobody is manipulating the switch. Employees have noticed the lights will be turned in the 'on' position upon arrival in the morning, when in fact, they had been turned 'off' the night before. With concern of a wiring or electrical issue, the technicians have verified there is no electrical problem.

Another store employee had such a frightening feeling

about the left-hand side, second story of the building, that she refused to go into the area, at all. Only accessing the Break Room, this individual would avoid the inventory and storage area at all costs, stating that they had sensed there was something "very bad" in that location.

Perhaps two of the most suspicious indications that the energies from 207 may have infiltrated the store, is the fact that several employees have expressed concerns about the shifting of the air inside the building, particularly on the left-hand side, second story. It has been described as a "heavy, somewhat uncomfortable, feeling." Additionally, the other disconcerting fact has to do with *several* former employees have been fired for fighting.

Listening to both employees describe the sudden onset of the fighting, was of special concern to me, given what I endured and witnessed while Jim and I lived at 207. Describing incidents where employees have just "snapped" and "attacked" other employees, or have become aggressive and hostile towards other associates without prompting, or basis of motivation, goes right along with the way Jim had acted at times, more specifically, and more frequently, in the last several months before his death. An unprecedented four (or five employees), have been terminated within a five-year span, prompting one of the store employees to remark that they have never "seen anything like it, before."

Long before my phone call to the store, Candace began conducting EVPs during her meal and break times. The EVPs were recorded in the Break Room, located on the second floor.

The first EVP was of a woman's voice stating, "Is anyone there?" A second, and separate EVP was that of a male voice asking, "Aren't you going to tell me your name?" In the background, a strange "electrical" interference could be heard on one of the recordings.

Candace apparently played the EVPs to coworkers, who were extremely curious as to whom they voices belonged to. It was at that point that she and the others nicknamed the male voice, "Henry," disregarding the female voice.

Ironically, neither one of us thought it was a mere coincidence, relative to the male and female energies. I personally, was amazed by the fact that she had been recording the EVPs, *before* my call.

I did advise Candace that there was quite a bit of evidence to suggest that at the very least, my husband Jim had experienced and suffered, a demonic oppression and possession. Corroborating Jim's death, the experiences at 207, as well as Ann Fisher's assessment, and Jerry's death, there was a high probability that the energies had impacted everyone's life, in one form or another.

Also discussed was a concern for the single residential property that exists a few lots west of 207. Even today, I have a strong sense that the resident(s) *may* have experienced activity. For this reason, and from my perspective, I would think that both the store and the residence would be prime locations to conduct a full-fledged paranormal investigation. Understanding basic corporate law relative to the commercial property, it seems very unlikely that the Corporate Office would allow one to take place in the store.

Candace did remark that she is on a friendly basis with one of the residents, who lives in the lone house. She suggested that the next time she were to see the customer, she would ask if the resident would be interested in speaking to me. I believe that it would be beneficial to the Homeowner to permit a complete investigation, and am interested to find out if they would be willing to have one conducted.

At the conclusion of that very long fact-finding conversation, I provided Candace with names and other pertinent information relating to the house's history. We both agreed that it would be useful "trigger" information while she continued to conduct the EVPs during her breaks.

Since the call, and as recent as early June 2011, the following new EVPs have been recorded:

Question: "Do you have anything to say to Jill?"

Answer: "She left me." (Male voice with a strong electrical interference occurring at the time of recording).

Question: "Is anyone there?"

Answer: "Here we go." (Male voice with another strong interference heard. The room lights also turned off, and then on, by themselves).

I do think that the male voice may be more indicative of the male spirit energy that had sporadically appeared, and kept watch over 207. I say this because I have no reason to think, nor have I sensed, the spirit of my husband to be at unrest. Considering that I did 'leave' before the wicked energies could do me any harm, I would have to correlate that specific EVP with the fact that I did leave 'him" – or it.

Noteworthy, is the fact that after referencing Internet mapping, I clearly identified the left-hand side of the new building is closest to the lot of 207. More oddly is the fact that Jim and I had lived in the second story flat, with the problem area of the store being located on the second story, left-hand side.

When Ann Fisher had asked me about the proximity of 207 in relationship to the nearest church, and had identified the second energy as that of a nun from the photos I had provided, it was quite interesting to know that Saint Patrick's Roman Catholic Church is just over three hundred feet west of 207's lot. There is something else that has factored into the theory about the nun...

Long before Jim took his life, I would remember looking out the kitchen window towards Len and Sarah's, and sensing that very negative presence off to the distance, in a northwesterly direction. For years, I had a niggling hunch.

From the onset of taking notice to the energy, I never tried to figure out what the problem was, and assumed that at one time or another, something bad had happened over in that general direction. Not until recent investigation into the local history, for sake of correlating the very broad and eclectic past of Watervliet, to 207, did I stumble onto some rather alarming information as to what may have taken place in the original house, as well as the immediate area.

Today, given the technological advances relative to 'zoom

tools' featured on Internet mapping services, I picked up on that same feeling when plugging in the old address and surveying the area: I sensed a direct connection between Saint Patrick's Church, and that dark, northwesterly location.

With years of honing my abilities now under my belt, I am highly sensitive to 'reading' energies, even at great distances and utilize the tool to assist me with spirit energy readings of client properties. I have been able to pick up on some very detailed information by doing so, and with that said, strongly believe that the energies which haunted 207, may very well have to do with something associated with both Saint Patrick's Church, and Saint Colman's Home. As for proximity to the flat, Saint Colman's Home is approximately 1.5 miles northwest of the lot, located on Haswell Road.

Continuing with the historical research, I have also come across some bothersome information pertaining to specific dates and individuals who lived, and worked in the very vicinity of 207, dating back as far as the early 19th Century. I have also found two old photographs that directly have bore incredible insight to the paranormal activity.

I will not include the date at this time, but will address all of the latest developments and historical aspects, in a sequel to this book, as my investigation continues to uncover a plethora of astounding information, connecting the events and energies, to the data. I will, however, state that the significance and emotional impact of seeing the two photographs, brought tears to my eyes, as I have discovered in them, what may very well be the catalyst for what has been almost two centuries of negative energy at 207.

As for the store: There will be more legwork to do relative to the activity that seems prevalent in that specific area. EVPs should continue to be conducted, and a blessing, and, or cleansing, has been strongly suggested.

Asked if I would go to the store to conduct a reading, as I often do as part of my business, I have declined. I have chosen to continue to take Ann Fisher's expert advice and stay off of the property, especially now knowing that the energies have drifted into the store. The same would apply to the single home that exists on the north side of 19th Street, a few lots west of 207.

Simply said, I cannot take a chance and place myself in harm's way. "It" wanted my son and I dead, and I implicitly state that I will not put either one of us in a situation that could make it more dangerous, or would facilitate an attachment given the history. Call me crazy, but if someone offered me a million, even ten million dollars to walk onto the property, I would refuse it. There are just some things that you cannot put a price on: The well-being and safety of my family and I, being number one.

People will criticize the events that I have shared in this book, but this entire saga has gone beyond coincidence and has prompted discussions amongst professionals in the paranormal community, inclusive of varying religious and spiritual communities. Looking at all of the evidence, it also appears that this story is sadly, far from over. As a Spiritual Medium and Clairvoyant, I am genuinely concerned for the immediate area surrounding the intersections of 19th and 2nd, and fear that the energies will continue to wreak havoc, until they are cast-out.

As previously mentioned, I have started to gather notes, along with the research data, to correlate the paranormal and demonic activity, with historical information for my next book. With my most recent investigation shedding new light onto a violent, and secretive past existing long before I had moved into the house during the early summer of 1988, it appears that the wicked forces of 207, still continue to case the neighborhood. The connection between the supernatural phenomenon and historical facts has identified an origin, and has demonstrated a strong cause for the demonic energies to swarm the corners of 19th Street, and 2nd Avenue.

Beyond a shadow of a doubt, a sad and tragic history lies cloaked by the daily hustle and bustle of Watervliet's busy, city streets. And whether carried by a sweltering summer breeze, or a chilly winter wind, the dark energies persist to lurk amidst the unsuspecting, seeking to feed upon the weak of heart, mind and – soul.

* * * * * * *

If you, or anyone you know of is suicidal, or has threatened suicide, please contact your nearest mental health facility, or call the National Suicide Prevention Lifeline at:
1-(800) 273-TALK(8255)

For more information, you may also visit:
www.suicidepreventionlifeline.org

Domestic Violence is a crime. If you are in need of help, please call The National Domestic Violence Hotline at:
1-(800) 799-SAFE(7233), or TTY 1-(800) 787-3224

For more information, you may also visit:
www.thehotline.org

A portion of proceeds from the sale of this book will be divided between, and donated to: The National Suicide Prevention Lifeline, and The National Domestic Violence Hotline. *Thank you.*

ABOUT THE AUTHOR

A native of Upstate New York, Jill Marie Morris is an Author, Designer, Spiritual Medium and Clairvoyant who uses her unique set of abilities to help others. She also is a Paranormal Investigator, and Researcher.

Collecting significant historical data during her research of the Albany area, Jill Marie will be authoring a sequel to "207," which will provide breadth to a series of startling revelations involving the history, relative to her experiences while living in Watervliet, New York, in the late 1980's.

Residing along the Gulf Coast of Florida, Jill Marie enjoys painting, sculpting, history, architecture, cooking, gardening, and travel. She also loves spending time with her family, and two very spoiled felines: Miss Zelda Bodeen and Master Merlin.

CPSIA information can be obtained at www.ICGtesting.com
Printed in the USA
LVOW121735210513

334859LV00015B/391/P

9 781463 550431